Relax,
It's Only
a Ghost!

Relax,
It's Only a Ghost!

My Adventures with Spirits,
Hauntings and Things
That Go Bump in the Night

ECHO L. BODINE

FAIR WINDS
PRESS

GLOUCESTER, MASSACHUSETTS

Fair Winds Press
33 Commercial Street
Gloucester, MA 01930

First paperback edition 2001

Library of Congress Cataloging-in-Publication data available.

Printed in Canada

ISBN 1-931412-71-5

Cover design: Michele Wetherbee
Cover illustration: Nicky Ovitt

Contents

Acknowledgments   xi

Preface   xiii

Introduction   xxvii

Chapter 1   What Is a Ghost?   1

Chapter 2   My First Ghostbusting   13

Chapter 3   My Second Encounter with a Ghost   18

Chapter 4   Who Ya Gonna Call?   26

Chapter 5   He Wanted the Kids Out of There   38

Chapter 6   He Was Afraid God Was Mad at Him   44

Chapter 7   The Ghost Was in Love   48

Chapter 8   "I Don't Want to See My Sister"   51

Chapter 9   A Policeman Named Bill   55

Chapter 10   The Ghosts Were Stoned   58

Chapter 11   She Was Bouncing Him off the Walls   61

Chapter 12   He Didn't Know He Was Dead   64

Chapter 13   His Kids Were Afraid to Sleep Over   68

Chapter 14   The Log Cabin in the Woods   75

Chapter 15   Bobby Mackey's Music World   87

Chapter 16   The Spirit Kept Entering His Body   104

Chapter 17   How to Get Rid of a Ghost   111

Afterword   123

To Christian

I Found a Ghost

The other day I found a ghost
lying up against the shoe trees in my closet.
If he planned to stay
I expected more than the usual wall thumping,
moans and groans, so often typical of his kind.
I suggested he clean up around the house
three days a week
and also help scare off any potential burglars.
He was definitely not impressed,
felt overburdened
and was worried about taking on such a
    heavy work load.
I then told him to get a life.

—Sam DiPaola

Acknowledgments

MANY, MANY thanks to the following people:

Caroline Pincus, whose wonderful title is Book Midwife. You certainly are that and more. You not only breathed new life into me with this book, but you brought the book alive with your wonderful creative talent, and I thank you from the bottom of my heart.

As always, I'd like to thank my wonderful family, the Bodines, who are always so supportive of my work, and a very special thank you to my brother and ghostbusting partner, Michael, who always protected me when I felt scared and made our time together on these jobs so special. Thanks, too, for your wonderful sense of humor. As hard as this work is, you always make me laugh.

My fiancé, Mike Hartley, for pushing me for three years not to give up on this project and for being my sounding board while I worked on each chapter.

Jonathon Lazear, my literary agent, not only for bringing Greg Brandenburgh and Element Books into my life but for coming up with the great title for this book.

Christi Cardenas for always returning my calls and calming my author anxieties.

Donna Guice for the hours and hours of typing you did on the original manuscript and for your excitement about this project.

Mike Warnell, my ghostbusting buddy, when my brother wasn't able to be there.

To all the ghosts who've taught me so much.

Preface

I SEE GHOSTS. I've seen them for almost thirty years. I've met a ghost who sings opera and a ghost named Mr. Peterson who paced back and forth in the basement of the house he built, trying to prevent the new owner from remodeling. I've seen a group of eight ghosts all huddled together on the bed of a little girl who had been complaining to her mommy that she couldn't sleep because of "all the people sleeping in her bed." I once encountered three Mexican ghosts who lived in an attic and appeared to the renter in her mirror.

I've worked with a female ghost named Sherrie who had been murdered and chose to stay here rather than face her killer—who had committed suicide—on the other side. I've seen a ghost roaming the halls of St. Paul City Hall in her wedding dress, waiting for her boyfriend to arrive so they could get married. I was once slapped on the back of my neck by a ghost who told me to get out of the warehouse he "worked in," and another ghost tried pushing me down the very stairs where she jumped to her death over a hundred years ago.

I've felt them walk through me and I've seen them come right up to my face and try to take my breath away (hoping to gain power from the energy).

I've seen them in people's garages, attics, showers, bedrooms, basements, kitchens. Sitting in chairs, lying on beds, pretending to dine at dinner tables, marching up and down hallways, acting as if they're sipping tea, staring out windows, riding elevators, sitting in classrooms, acting on stage, being in the audience on a TV show.

Ghosts are in homes, churches, businesses, hospitals, school dorms, libraries, tanning parlors, farms, funeral homes, treatment centers, cabins, flower shops, day care centers. Anywhere that people hang out, ghosts hang out too.

The two most rewarding aspects of being a ghostbuster are knowing that I've helped another soul move on to begin a new life and knowing that I've brought peace of mind to a homeowner who's been living with uninvited guests.

About a year ago, I had a reading from a psychic (yes, psychics get readings too!) who told me that there were many souls from the other side who wanted to thank me for helping them move on; he then gave me several of their names. As he listed their names, I remembered each one of them and the particular ghostbusting it entailed. It brought tears to my eyes, knowing that these souls who had resisted moving on for so long were now at peace.

Working with ghosts definitely has its ups and downs. It takes a lot of physical energy to do ghost-bustings. When I go into someone's home, office, or school to locate ghosts, I have to open up psychically as much as possible in order to see and hear them. They have a very light energy, and it takes quite a bit of energy to communicate at their level.

It's tough to explain, but I want to try to help you understand this as much as possible. We humans have a dense energy. We're heavy. Our vibration or energy is heavy. A soul or spirit is lighter than a feather. In order to connect with them we have to raise our energy level to that very light vibration, and that can be very draining physically.

I recently interviewed the medium James Van Praagh for a local newspaper in the Twin Cities called *The Edge.* While sitting next to James, I could feel how light his energy was, something I had never felt with anyone living. When I asked him how he got his vibration so light, he told me it was through years of meditating. For many years, watching him work on TV, I had wondered how he was able to bring through such intimate details from deceased loved ones on the other side, and now I understood that he had disciplined himself to raise his vibration to their level and maintain himself at that level.

For me, I go back and forth, functioning from the heavier level here on earth, working with the homeowner and his or her friends and neighbors, and then raising myself up to the lighter energy of the spirits. If we just had to go in and take care of the ghosts, the work wouldn't be so exhausting, but we usually need to spend equal time with the homeowners, helping them understand what's going on, and I believe it's the going back and forth between the two energies that's so tiring.

In the last few years, I've finally gotten smart and I bring either my secretary or my good friend Mike Warnell along on the job. They take care of explaining to the homeowners what's going on and answer all their questions, while I do my work. It's a lot less physically draining this way.

Another reason it's nice to have an assistant along is that we can focus our psychic abilities on the ghosts rather than on trying to block ourselves from picking up information on the people in the room. When we're as opened up psychically as we need to be, it's not uncommon to pick up info on everyone around us, and that in itself can be pretty distracting. We really don't want to know about the spouse who's having the extramarital affair or the health problems in someone's body, or feel the animosity coming from the skeptics in the room.

After we've gotten the ghosts out of there and into

the light, we do enjoy talking to the people, answering their questions and alleviating their fears. That's the second most gratifying part of the job, when we can tell people that everything's okay and that they're now the only ones living in their homes.

Whenever we leave a job, we're always starving, so we head for a fast-food drive-through and load up on food to help replenish our energy and ground our bodies. I always sleep at least ten to twelve hours after a ghostbusting job.

Over the years many of the students in my psychic development classes have voiced a desire to become ghostbusters, and frankly my first inclination is to talk them out of it. Besides being physically draining, it isn't the kind of occupation that can be counted on to put food on the table. Calls seem to come in waves, and, contrary to popular belief, there aren't more calls at Halloween than at other times of the year! We get between two and eight calls per month. As you can imagine, many of our clients don't have money set aside in their budgets for ghost exterminators, so there have been many times when we've driven away from a job with just enough money to pay for our burgers and fries.

Many clients do pay for our services (around $100, which we split), but money has definitely not been our reason for doing this work. It's about helping souls find their way home and bringing peace of mind to people on this side of the light.

One of the most fun aspects of being a ghost-buster has been working with the media. I've been on some great radio and TV shows over the years: *Sally Jesse Raphael, Sightings, Encounters,* NBC's *The Other Side,* and the *Tom Barnard Show,* to name a few. And I've been interviewed by some very cool magazines, too. In April 1992, my brother and I were on the cover of *Corporate Report,* with a great article written about our abilities, called "Otherworldly Entrepreneurs." Working with the media has given us a great venue for educating people about ghosts and life after death, and fortunately for me, most of the experiences have been positive.

Once in a while I have a negative experience with a radio announcer who thinks he's got a right to be rude to me because I have these abilities, or who insinuates that I (or anyone in my profession) must be a con artist or fraud. That's been the most hurtful part of my career as a psychic and ghostbuster. Usually, after the first five or ten minutes, a reporter or producer will realize that I have integrity and that my intentions are honorable, but in the beginning of every meeting, whether it's to do an interview or a show, I get the unspoken message that I have to prove myself. On the one hand, I understand it because there are a lot of frauds out there (as in any profession), but on the other hand, after doing this work for over thirty years, it's gotten old!

• • •

People always ask me if I see ghosts all the time or only when I'm on a job, and the answer is that for the most part I only see them when I'm at a ghost-busting job. But once in a while, when I'm in a relaxed state, I do see ghosts. Here are a couple of examples:

Two years ago, my fiancé and I went to a bed and breakfast for his birthday. The owner told me that there were menus of all the area restaurants in the sitting room, so I went in to check them out—and there, sitting about a foot above the couch, was the spirit of a young man. He looked up at me and I smiled at him, which startled him. He told me he had died in Vietnam and that this was his hometown. Seemed like a nice enough fellow, and after reminding myself that I was there to relax, not work, I left the room and went back to ours. I told my fiancé, who got that sort of blank Lutheran stare he gets whenever I mention spotting a ghost.

We didn't talk about it again until the next morning at breakfast, when I asked the owner of the B&B if she was aware of any ghosts in the house. She said people would mention from time to time that they'd seen the apparition of a young man, but she said she'd never seen him herself.

If he had seemed like a tormented soul, I probably would have pushed the idea of helping him move on to the other side, but he seemed content and the owner said nothing about getting rid of him, so I let it go.

Another incident that comes to mind happened in 1995. I flew out to L.A. to be a guest on the *Mike and Maty Show,* and they put me up in the Roosevelt Hotel. It was the night before the taping, and I was lying in bed watching television. All of a sudden a male spirit came rushing through the wall into the room, followed by a female spirit. They looked as if they were playing chase or hide and go seek. Of course, my heart was up in my throat in about two seconds, because I was relaxing and wasn't expecting company.

Finding a way to live with both of my realities has definitely been one of the most challenging aspects of my work and my life path. It can get pretty weird sometimes. There was this one evening, several years ago, when my mother-in-law came for dinner. I was in the kitchen preparing hamburgers for the grill and was also engaged in a conversation with my (then) husband and his mom. Suddenly my best friend, Joanie, who had died two years earlier, appeared to me and started talking to me.

I first heard her voice say, "Hi buddy," which is what she called me when she was living, but it took me a couple of seconds to recognize her soul. She looked so much younger than forty-two, her age when her body died. She wasn't wearing the glasses she always wore, her hair was still light brown, and she appeared to be much thinner than when she was in the body, but there was such a familiar feeling when I looked at her that I knew it was someone dear to me.

I looked at my husband to see if he could see her, and could tell by the look on his face that he was totally oblivious to her presence. It's just one of those situations I find myself in quite often where there are two completely different realities going on for me at the same time.

I sent a quick thought to Joanie to meet me out by the barbecue grill, grabbed the hamburgers, and excused myself. The whole time the burgers were cooking, I stood outside and had a conversation with my friend. I don't know why she chose to show up at that particular time. Oftentimes when spirits have something on their mind, they want to deal with it right then, and they act oblivious to what's going on in our lives. They come, they say it, they're gone. It's that simple for them.

Then there was the time about a year or so ago when my fiancé and I were just sitting down to Sunday night dinner. I felt a cold breeze walk through me, and I knew a spirit was in the room and wanted to communicate with me. I really wasn't in the mood and just wanted to have a nice peaceful dinner, so I tried ignoring the feeling, but then an image of a woman's face appeared right in front of me. I figured

I'd better open up my third eye, which I do by visualizing an opening at the top of my head, and find out what was going on so that I could deal with it and get on with my dinner. It turned out to be my fiancé's aunt, who had died exactly one year ago that day. She wanted me to give her husband a message, so I grabbed a piece of paper and wrote it down, then she thanked me and left. I shut off my third eye (by visualizing the opening at the top of my head closed up) and ate my dinner while I explained to my boyfriend what had just happened. It was one of those "I just talked to your deceased aunt, please pass the mashed potatoes" episodes. That's what I mean when I say my biggest struggle is learning how to live in both worlds at the same time and carry on a normal life without upsetting the people around me.

My fiancé and I have this running joke. I kiddingly tell him I think he should wear a bell when he's walking around the house because we have carpeting on all the floors and I can never hear when he's coming into the room. I only see something moving toward me out of the corner of my eye, and because it's so quiet, I usually assume it's a materialized spirit of some kind —either a guardian angel, spirit guide, or deceased relative. Either way, I end up jumping about three feet in the air *every time* he comes into a room, simply because I never know who it's going to be!

Of all the different aspects of my work, such as psychic readings, spiritual healing, teaching classes, writing books, and clearing homes of unwanted spirits, "ghostbusting" is by far the topic most people are curious about. They want to know what ghosts are, what they look like, if they can harm us. They want to know why ghosts haunt our homes and, of course, the big question: how to get rid of them.

This wasn't always the case. For a long time people didn't want to hear about ghosts. They were content with *Casper the Friendly Ghost* comics. But then Hollywood got creative and came up with movies like *The Exorcist* and *Poltergeist*. Those two movies alone kept most of us scared for years and also provided some very funny material for stand-up comics.

Then in 1990, the movie *Ghost* came out, and we all stopped sleeping with our lights on. Finally Hollywood gave us something realistic to look at as far as ghosts, spirit communication, and life after death are concerned. I think I saw that movie half a dozen times, I loved it so much. What was even more wonderful about it was that it got people talking and asking questions. People's consciousness started changing about death and life after death. Then we got more wonderful movies like *Always,* which *fairly accurately* teaches us about the role spirit guides play in our life and the importance of letting go, and *Defending Your Life,* which gives us a look at the whole concept of life review, something that we all do after death. And in 1999, we had the hit movie *The Sixth Sense,* a totally cool movie about a little boy who can see dead people and the therapist who helps him cope with his abilities. If you haven't seen these movies, I highly recommend that you do because each of them gives us another piece to the big puzzle.

The simple fact is this: ghosts are stuck souls. The "busting" part of ghostbusting is helping set them free. As we know from people who've had near-death experiences, there is a tunnel where many of our deceased loved ones are waiting for us. The end of the tunnel, which is the entrance to the other side, is lit up by a beautiful white light. Our souls call this "home." My job as a ghostbuster is to get souls unstuck and move them into this light.

This book takes you along on numerous actual "ghostbustings" that I have done either by myself, with a student, or with my psychic brother, Michael. In these stories you'll see that ghosts are as unique as people and that each has his or her own personal reasons for remaining here on earth. I also share with you how we were able to get each one of them to move on to the other side. I wrote this book to bring you the truth about ghosts as seen through the eyes of a real-life ghosthunter!

Perhaps some of you have seen ghosts, but nobody believes you. Maybe *you* don't believe you and think you're going crazy! Through the stories in *Relax, It's Only a Ghost!*, I hope to give you some good tips on dealing with the ghosts in your lives. My purpose in writing it was to show you that you are not alone and that you really have nothing to fear. (I did put in some of the more entertaining parts of these real-life ghost stories simply because no matter what age we are, most of us still love to be scared by a good ghost story.)

Of course, if you've got a pesky ghost and you can't get rid of it even after reading the last chapter, you might want to call your local New Age bookstore and ask for a referral to a *reputable* ghostbuster or psychic in your area. Please note that not all psychics know how to work with ghosts, so make sure to ask them for references of other ghost clearings they've done before investing a lot of time and money in their services.

In the meantime, relax and enjoy as I take you along on my adventures in the world of ghosts. Each story you read is as close to accurate as possible, except that the names have been changed.

Introduction

IT WAS JUST a typical evening at our house in the fall of 1965, when I was seventeen. Sitting around the table after dinner were my parents, my two brothers, my sister and I. My brother said he was going downstairs to practice on his new drum set. He was just beginning to learn how to play the drums, so, needless to say, his playing still sounded a little rough. The rest of us were carrying on with our different after-dinner conversations, obviously trying to avoid the dishes for as long as possible, when—all of a sudden, as if on cue—everyone stopped talking. It was the music coming from the den downstairs. It was really good, not the usual beginner stuff we were used to hearing. We all looked at dad, expecting he would know why my brother suddenly sounded like an old pro. He said that it must be the new Sandy Nelson record he had just bought him, and, even though that answer didn't feel accurate, we went back to our conversations, continuing to listen for signs of what was really going on in the basement.

About a minute later, my brother came flying up

the stairs, hysterical, pale, and barely able to speak. My mom tried to calm him down. He looked so shaken, the entire family was scared. Finally he was able to settle down enough to talk. "Did you hear it, did you hear it?" he said, and we all answered, "Yes, wasn't it a record?" Still shaking, he said, "NO, it wasn't a record. I was sitting there practicing like always, when out of nowhere, a white figure floated through the door and over to me." He went on to say that he closed his eyes really tight, hoping it would disappear, but even with his eyes closed, he could still see this whitish male figure standing in front of the drum set. He said this guy took his hands and basically played through him, making the really beautiful music. He struggled to let go of the drumsticks and, as soon as he could get his hands free, he ran out of the room and upstairs. He was so upset, he said he was never going down to the den again.

We were all stunned and scared ourselves. My mom, who usually kept a cool head, said she was going to call a woman in her prayer group who knew of a medium from England who was living in St. Paul. Mom said the woman in her group was a good person and would know what to do.

As if all this weren't eerie enough, when mom called the medium, a woman named Mrs. Olson, she told my mother she'd been expecting the call. After my mother related the story of what had happened with my brother and the drumming, Mrs. Olson told her that the spirit was my brother's guardian angel, Dr. Fitzgerald. When this doctor was living on earth, he was also a drummer, and besides being my brother's angel, he was going to work with him through the drums. She also told mom that each one of us (mom and us four kids) had some very unique gifts and that she wanted to see everyone for a session. We were all so blown away. What did all of this mean? Did we all have guardian angels? Why could my brother see his, when the rest of us couldn't see anything? Should we tell our friends or keep this a family secret? My poor parents were so inundated with questions from the four of us that they had no clue how to answer. I was so frightened by the thought that my own guardian angel might appear to me that that night I began sleeping with the lights on.

Within a week my mom began taking each one of us to see Mrs. Olson.

On the drive from our south suburban home to her home in west St. Paul, I was full of anticipation. I wondered what this medium from England would be like. Was she like the psychics I had seen in the movies? Did she read a crystal ball? Was her house filled with black cats? Did she wear big dangling earrings and tie long scarves around her head? I was also curious about what she would tell me. At that point in my life, the only things I was interested in were meeting Mr. Right and wondering how many children I was going to have.

As we approached her front door, my stomach was in absolute butterflies. I felt so much fear, I just wanted to go away and pretend all of this wasn't happening. I told mom I wanted to go home. Much to my surprise, this very sweet, petite, round woman with an English accent answered the door and invited us in. She seemed so normal. There were no black cats or crystal balls. She introduced us to her very normal-looking husband and told my mother to have a seat in the living room while she escorted me into her "reading room."

When she began reassuring me that nothing frightening was going to happen, I wondered if everyone was so nervous on their first visit or if she was just being psychic and knew how scared I felt. She explained to me that the glass of water on her table was for the spirits. She said it gave them energy. Then she explained that the lump protruding from her forehead was where her third eye was, and that that was where she received her psychic information. She also said that my spirit guides, who were supposedly helpers from the other side, were the source from which she was getting her information on me.

I sat somewhat frozen in my chair, waiting for something to fly through the room or a spirit to manifest itself, neither of which, thankfully, happened.

Instead, this very gentle medium from England told me that I had psychic abilities—clairvoyance, the gift of psychic sight, and clairaudience, the ability to hear spirit—and that I had the gift of healing. I was totally stunned as she told me that I had come here in this lifetime to be a well-known psychic and spiritual healer. I would write books, be on TV and radio, travel and teach others how to develop their abilities, and I would be known throughout the world.

I was a shy teenager at the time and couldn't imagine myself being famous. I had plans of going to college to become a social worker and had always imagined myself as a wife and mother someday. I told Mrs. Olson I was going to college and that I didn't think I had any psychic abilities. She told me that I had been hearing voices all my life and was so used to it that I didn't give it much thought. She also said that I did not come here in this lifetime to have a normal life and that I came to be a teacher.

Something inside of me knew that what she was saying was true, but I pretended not to know it because it all seemed so scary and totally out of my reality. I didn't know how to think about it.

In my mother's reading, Mrs. Olson told her that she was also very gifted psychically and would use her abilities to help people as well.

After that first session with Mrs. Olson, mom and I became very curious about our abilities. We went to occult bookstores (it was the sixties) and started reading whatever was available. We bought a Ouija board, and our home slowly became a haven for mischievous, noisy spirits. They would bang on the walls or make footstep sounds or the sound of someone typing on a typewriter. Life was becoming scary for all of us. We never knew what to expect. It was as if we had opened a door to something we didn't understand and we couldn't get the door closed.

One night when we were all sitting around the dinner table, we could hear voices coming from upstairs in my bedroom, calling my name. It was a creepy, wailing kind of sound, with several voices calling, "Echo, come here, come here." We were scared to death as we went upstairs to investigate and realized the voices were actually coming from the Ouija board. We called Mrs. Olson and asked her what we should do, and she advised us to burn the board in the fireplace immediately. We had become almost addicted to that board, asking it questions about everything in our lives. It seemed almost cruel to burn it, so mom took it out to the trash cans, which were at least twenty feet from the house. The next morning when we came down for breakfast, there it was, sitting on the kitchen table. It scared us so much that we immediately burned the board and, much to our surprise, the moaning sounds we had heard periodically throughout the house stopped!

Spirit activity didn't stop though. We continued to have psychic experiences almost daily. My younger brother, Michael, could see and hear spirits. Even my sister, Nikki, who was oblivious to most of the supernatural goings-on in the house, saw a spirit before I did. Lights blinked on and off. Radios and TVs would come on and turn off by themselves. Things were moved from room to room. The stuffed animals in my bedroom would move by themselves. We always had a feeling of being watched.

There was one night in particular that I will never forget. My parents had gone away for the weekend, and this guy I was dating stopped by. He had been drinking and was coming on to me very aggressively. I felt afraid because I was the only one home at the time and couldn't get him to stop. I silently asked the spirits in the house to do something to get him out of there. No sooner had I asked than the broom closet door opened all by itself. Out of the closet came the broom, floating a good three feet off the ground. It moved through the entire length of the room we were in, then returned to the closet and fell on the floor. My intoxicated friend was out of there faster than you could say "poltergeist."

Sometime during the first year of all of this, a psychic, spiritualist minister in Minneapolis called my mom. The minister said that her spirit guides had told her to teach us how to develop our psychic abilities. She said there were eight people in all who would be attending these classes and that we were to start in one week.

We were so freaked out by everything going on already, we weren't sure how much more involved we wanted to get, but we decided to go the first night just to see what it was all about. We were pleasantly surprised to find that everyone else in class seemed as normal as we were and had all the same uncertainties that we had. We ended up going to these classes on and off for close to two years.

I can't really say I took to psychic development like a duck takes to water. It took me a long time to develop my abilities fully because I let my intellect get in the way most of the time. I analyzed all the psychic information that came to me, and I questioned everything that my teacher said. I was looking for something concrete I could hold onto. I wanted it to all make sense on a rational level. Letting go of my mainstream thinking, and believing and accepting things that couldn't be seen by the human eye or proven by science, was very scary for me. I would say that my skepticism made my psychic development a lot harder than it had to be, but I'm glad I was as skeptical as I was. I didn't buy everything hook, line and sinker; I acquired new beliefs only slowly and because I had studied them.

Take spirit guides, for example. Mrs. Olson or my

teacher Birdie might say there were spirit guides, but that didn't convince me they existed. I told my guides that if they were really there, I needed them to somehow make themselves known to me. It took a while for me to feel the connection. After "feeling" their presence, I was able to hear them talking to me. The male guide told me his name was Theodore but I could call him Teddy. The female guide said her name was Anna. After I became comfortable conversing with them, then I began to see them. My mom and brother Michael were more accepting of their gifts, less skeptical, but for me the whole process of developing my abilities has happened one step at a time.

It's been thirty-four years since Mrs. Olson first told me about my abilities, and I would say that as each year has passed, it's gotten easier to live with my gifts. I've worked hard to maintain a pretty normal lifestyle. I don't dress, act or play the role a lot of people expect me to play when they find out I have these abilities. One of the things I talked to God about way back in the beginning of my career was that if this was really what he wanted me to do, I would do it, but I needed him with me at all times to guide me in my work and in my life. I've worked hard at developing my relationship with God and living a spiritual path.

When I started doing ghosthunting over thirty

years ago, I never would have guessed that it would become such an important part of my life and work. I hope the stories that follow will not only entertain you but give you some genuine insight and compassion for the stuck souls we call ghosts.

CHAPTER ONE

What Is a Ghost?

IT WAS A dark and stormy night. The thunder shook the trees from their very roots. Bolts of lightning struck the earth's surface, burning holes deep into the soil.

What was inside the house was ten times as frightening. The Livingstons had ghosts. Several black, monstrous floating creatures. They would knock lamps off tables, push pictures off walls, throw clothes out of the closets and drawers. They killed the family dog, Fluffy, and ate the guinea pig, Hector. The cat spewed brown foam from its mouth and moaned incessantly. The Livingstons wanted to know when this reign of terror was going to stop.

Green smoke would burn out of the nostrils of these unwelcome guests. Their red eyes glared in the dark. Purple slime dripped from their mouths. Nothing could stop or tame these horrible visitors from the world beyond. They were out to destroy the family home and drive Mr. and Mrs. Livingston insane. They hated with a vengeance. They showed no mercy on the children the day they tied them up and chopped off their toes. They were horrible, villainous monsters slowly taking over and destroying this beautiful nineteenth-century Victorian home.

Just as an evil-looking specter looms toward Mr. Livingston wielding a bloody ax, someone in the back room hollers, "Cut, let's do that scene over," and we realize it's Hollywood making another movie about ghosts!

Like most people, I grew up around a television set, and so when the subject of ghosts would come up, all I could think of were these TV images. I had no idea what a ghost *really* was or looked like. I had this belief that they were all evil except for dear, sweet Casper, who was the only friendly ghost I had ever heard of.

Over the years I've noticed that most people share these misconceptions about ghosts: Ghosts are to be feared and not reckoned with. They are all evil spirits who will cause great harm to anyone whose house is haunted or who comes in contact with them.

As a person who has the ability to hear and see ghosts, I can tell you that ghosts are nothing like the images on TV.

When we physically die, our souls come out of our bodies, and, most of the time, we move on to the other side. Once in a while a soul will choose, for one reason or another, not to go on to the other side (more on that below). It will choose to stay here on earth, which is where the term "earthbound" spirit or ghost comes from.

A soul is made up of energy. It looks like the physical body it inhabited except that it's transparent. Some parapsychologists call the soul *the body double* because it does look so much like the physical body that it inhabited in its last life, but I have also seen the soul appear as a streak of light or blob of energy. When a soul appears in body form, it will also appear to have on clothing similar to something the person wore when in the body. A friend of mine who was killed visited me a few times after his death, and he always appeared to have on the same blue jeans and camel-colored leather jacket that he frequently wore when he was alive. My teacher told us that they do this so they won't frighten us, just in case we are able to see them.

Psychically, I saw the comedian Sam Kinnison about one week after he died, walking around on the other side shaking people's hands. He appeared to be wearing his long coat, tennis shoes, and that hat he always wore in his comedy routine. If he had been walking around in a flowing gown, I don't think I would have recognized him. Also common, and a little eerie, is that they will sometimes only appear from the waist up or as just a head! This is because their energy is low and that's all they are able to manifest. It doesn't mean they're not all there—it just means that's as visible as they can make themselves at that time. As time passes, they will build up their energy and be able to appear in full form.

Why Ghosts Hang Around

I bet you're wondering why ghosts would choose not to go on to the other side. In my work, I've come to see that there are seven levels of souls. Souls at levels one and two are new souls. They are at the beginning stages of their development and haven't yet grasped the meaning of life and the significance of the other side. As they mature and move into levels three and four, they have a greater understanding of what life and death and life after death are all about. It is my view that ghosts are level-one and level-two souls, although I have met an occasional ghost who is more mature and simply sticking around to care for someone (more on that later). Level-three and level-four souls have been around enough times to know about the light and the importance of moving into it and getting on with their journeys.

• • •

Here's what the ghosts have taught me about what's keeping them stuck on this plane:

- They are afraid to face God because of some things they did in their life. They were taught that God is a punishing God, and they fear that they will be sent to hell for their "bad deeds," so instead of going over and taking that chance, they stay here. They actually believe that God can't find them as long as they don't cross over!

- There is someone they do not like who has died, and they don't want to run into them in heaven. Many a ghost has told us they don't want to run into their deceased ex-husband or ex-wife and that they would rather stay here.

- They think going to heaven is going to be a real drag. They think they will automatically become angels and all the "fun in their life" will stop, so they decide to stay here and hang out with people who like to have a good time.

- They are afraid of letting go of their identity. They may have been someone important in their community and they want to stay here and "hold onto their name."

- Some ghosts don't know they are dead! That's right. Some of them believe there is no such thing as life after death, so when their body dies and their soul comes out of the body, they don't know where to go. If an angel, spirit guide or a deceased relative approaches them and tries to direct them over to heaven, they think they are hallucinating so they don't pay attention. They figure they couldn't possibly be dead because they feel so alive, and so they look around for a home to inhabit.

- They feel the strong pull of a loved one on this side, so they stay, thinking they are helping them in their grieving process.

- They stay to protect a loved one here.

- They don't want to leave a loved one.

- If they were murdered, they may stick around until justice has been served.

- If they died from addiction, they may hang around looking for a body to inhabit so they can continue their drug of choice.

- They don't feel worthy of going to heaven, so they stay put.

About a year ago I was giving a lecture to a large group of senior citizens on the subject of death and life after death. One woman in the audience told me she strongly disagreed with me about souls not going to heaven and said that we are God's property once we die and that God decides what he will do with us at the time of death. However, it has been explained to me by my spirit guides that we are given free will in death, just as we are given free will in life. We make the decisions for ourselves and are responsible for those decisions.

A question I'm asked every time I give a lecture on this subject is "Why don't spirit guides, angels or deceased loved ones living on the other side intervene and direct these earthbound souls home to heaven?"

There are many workers from the other side who do work with earthbound souls to help them "come home" (see my discussion of the Squadron, p. 118). I think that's why we don't have as many ghosts as we could have. The ghosts we encounter are the diehards—the stubborn, want-to-do-things-their-own-way kind of folks who will hold out until someone like us comes in and insists that they go. As you will see when you read each ghost story, each situation is so different.

Here's the routine that my brother Michael and I have found works best when doing these ghostbusting jobs:

When we first arrive, we sit with the people for a while, ask them what symptoms they're having that makes them think they have a ghost. We want to eliminate the usual sounds, like houses settling or noisy pipes.

Then we walk through each room of the house, preferably with no lights on, because this is less distracting and also makes it easier to see the ghosts, who give off a light grayish energy. We make notes of the rooms we find the ghosts in, and then once we've gone through the entire house, we go back to the rooms inhabited by a ghost and begin a dialogue with it.

We ask what their name is and why they're here. We explain that we're here to get them to move on to the other side and tell them it's important to get unstuck and move on with their life after death.

This is where most of the work takes place, especially if the ghost doesn't want to go. Our guides assist us, always giving us suggestions as to how to deal with each ghost. We carry on regular, out-loud conversations with the ghost, so that the client knows what's going on. After we convince the earthbound spirit to leave, we direct it to float to the tunnel, then through it, going toward the light. We both hear and see the ghost and know each step it's taking. We continually encourage it to move into the light, until it does.

Then we burn sage (burning sage is a Native American cleansing ritual) to clear the home of any negative energy left behind from the ghost, or fear or anger coming from the clients because of the ghost's activities.

How You Can Tell If You Have a Ghost

You might be wondering how you can tell if you have a ghost. First, you should know there's rarely only one ghost in a house; if there's one ghost, you can bet there are more. One reason for this is that ghosts will look for a house that already has some earth-bound spirits in it, so that they don't feel so alone. But though they may choose a house to live in that has other ghosts, they don't necessarily hang out with each other. They are always aware of each other but don't always "socialize." If they weren't much on socializing when living in a body, they often just continue on that way in death. But the fact that they want to be left alone doesn't mean they don't get lonely, so they hang out in houses that have other ghosts. We have, on occasion, found a home that has only one ghost, and that ghost usually wants to be left alone.

Here are the most common clues that you've got a ghost:

- Tapping or knocking on the walls
- Doorbell ringing when no one is there
- Radio and/or television going on and off by itself
- The sound of footsteps
- Sounds of breathing

- Water faucets being turned on by themselves

- Voices are heard, and no one is there.

- Music is heard with no obvious source playing it.

- Books or other objects being knocked off shelves

- Clothes thrown out of closets

- Wastepaper baskets turned upside down

- Burners turned on on the stove

- A definite cold spot in the room and no draft or window nearby

- Material possessions moved from room to room

- A white or grayish hazy object floating through a room

- Something touches you but no one is there.

- A feeling of someone sitting down on your couch or bed

- Children claiming they can see someone that you can't

- Something pulling your hair or tugging on your clothes

- Your house has been for sale for a long time and no one will buy it.

This last symptom is an interesting one. Over the years we have been called by several realtors who have done everything they could to sell a home and nothing was happening. In each case, when we came to check things out we found a ghost living in the home, and the ghost did not want anyone buying the house. In one situation, the original builder of the house had died and didn't want any new people moving in. He liked the current tenants. In another situation the ghost just wanted the place to himself, and in yet another the ghost was in love with the current homeowner and he didn't want her to move (see Chapter 7).

In each case we were able to get the ghost to move on (more about that later) and the house sold within a week.

Ghosts are as varied as people are. Some are angry, some are frightened, some are depressed, some are party animals who don't want to give up their good times. Just remember, we are in death as we were in life. Most of us will move on to the other side when our time comes. The souls that stay behind are a small number compared to the ones that move on.

This notion about all ghosts being evil is not based in reality. In order for a ghost to be evil, he would have had to be evil in his recent life—which of course is possible, but there are not as many evil people running around as some of the ghosthunters would lead you to believe. The majority of ghosts are simply unhappy, restless and harmless. Always remember when dealing with a ghost that you are the one with the body. You are the one with the power. Don't give it away.

Facts About Ghosts

The difference between a ghost and a spirit is very simple. They are both souls that are no longer living in a body, but a ghost is a soul that has remained on earth, and a spirit is a soul that has moved on to the other side and has begun a new life there. A spirit can come to this side to visit, but it will return home; spirits are not stuck here on Earth. Ghosts are.

CHAPTER TWO

My First Ghostbusting

IT WAS wintertime, 1969. I was twenty-one years old and still living at home. We'd had a lot of spirit activity in our house since getting on this path, but up until this point I hadn't actually *seen* any spirits.

The first time I ever went to someone's house intentionally looking for a ghost, I had no idea what I was doing. I was pretty scared and still in the mind-set that ghosts were scary monsters who looked all whitish and weird—like they had no form and were just blobs of scary stuff!

What made this fun was that it was a friend of my mom's who suspected she had a ghost, so mom and I went on this "job" together. The drive over to Carol's that night felt a lot like that drive over to Mrs. Olson's: we didn't know what to expect, and our imaginations were running wild. Carol had told us that there were strange sounds coming from the attic and a feeling as if someone were watching her family. She said that her son was a recovering alcoholic and was having a terrible time staying sober. She wondered if there was some kind of negative influence in the house preventing her son from maintaining his sobriety. She also said they could hear a choir singing church music, which was interesting because their home had at one time been a church.

On the drive over, I was full of questions for my mom. What were we looking for? Did Carol really think she might have a ghost? What did a ghost look like? What were we going to do if we found one? I thought we should probably turn around and go home. Finding ghosts was not something I wanted to do.

When we pulled up to her house, I imagined seeing scary things in all the windows. I was sure they were all watching me, ready to pounce on me as soon as I walked in the door. As usual, mom was pretty calm, which always helped me feel more grounded. We kidded around with Carol for a while, trying to lighten things up. Looking back, we were probably just stalling, because I don't think any of us really wanted to go to the attic and deal with whatever was there. The analytical part of me thought it was probably just noisy pipes and that there was nothing to make a fuss about.

Chitchat ended and it was time to see what was

up in the attic. Slowly we made our way up the stairs. I'm sure I had one eye open and the other one closed as we reached the top of the stairs. I had myself scared silly.

At first glance everything seemed normal. The usual boxes and stored furniture were there. Slowly, images began coming into focus. At first all I saw was a very faint image of a family of four standing across the room from us. It was quite strange to look at this almost invisible family. They looked so strained and old, so frightened. My rational mind was in there right away trying to explain it all away. I told myself I was making it up. That ghosts weren't people. Ghosts didn't look like that. They were supposed to be scary looking. These were simply transparent people who didn't look scary at all. Just tired, old and afraid.

They had a gray appearance to them. The man looked crabby and seemed angry that we were able to see them. The woman started talking to us as soon as she realized we could see her. I'm sure my mouth was hanging wide open as I watched this transparent female tell us about her death and explain that she was trapped in this house by her husband. She said he had been an alcoholic and a smoker. He had passed out one night after drinking and his cigarette burned their house down, and all four people perished in the fire. She said that her husband would not let any of them go on to the other side because he was afraid of being punished by God for killing his family. I was flabbergasted.

I looked at mom and could tell by the shocked look on her face that she had heard this woman as well. I asked her what we should do, and we came up with the idea to just tell them they couldn't stay at Carol's house. They had to leave because they were frightening Carol's family. Mom got some psychic information that the male spirit had been entering Carol's son's body from time to time in order to taste alcohol and cigarettes, and that was why it was difficult for her son to maintain sobriety. After telling them they needed to leave, we were anxious to leave, too. This was all so creepy. We had no idea what we were doing or how to get rid of them. They did disappear, giving us the illusion that they had left, but my guess is that they probably just stepped outside or went over to the neighbors' to make us think they were gone. We didn't see a church choir or any other spirits as we walked through the rest of the house. I think our fear shut us down psychically. There certainly was a feeling that there were more spirits there than we cared to know about, but I just wanted to go home. I wasn't ready to deal with ghosts yet!

Facts About Ghosts

The female ghost could have taken her children and moved on to the other side anytime she wanted, but she allowed her husband to control her in death as she undoubtedly had in life. Every one of us has to discover our own power at some point in our soul's development and stop giving it away to others. It's part of setting ourselves free.

CHAPTER THREE

My Second Encounter with a Ghost

THE NEXT TIME we went to class, Mom and I told our teacher Birdie what had happened at Carol's, and she told us that in the future we shouldn't show any fear because the spirits can draw on our fear energy and make themselves bigger. She said that if ever we're around spirits and feel afraid, we should say a prayer, such as the Lord's Prayer, to help us feel more in control. As she was saying all this, I told myself it didn't matter because I had no intention of going to any more haunted houses. Little did I know that shortly thereafter the advice would come in very handy.

One evening after my church youth group meeting, Dean, one of the guys in the group, told me he had heard through the grapevine that I had psychic abilities. He wanted to know if I would come over and check out his attic because there were sounds of footsteps and strange noises that neither he nor his roommates could explain. He said that every day when they came home from work, they would find one of their baby kittens dead, crushed by something heavy. All I could think about was Birdie's advice about not showing fear when dealing with a spirit. I wondered if I was strong enough to go see what was killing their kittens, and I told Dean that even though I wasn't very experienced in this area, I would give it a try.

Our whole youth group excitedly piled into cars and took off for his house. I wanted to help but I also felt a lot of fear about what I was walking into. I asked my spirit guides to help me, but I wasn't too good at hearing them yet.

On the drive over I found myself trying to explain to myself, what the noises might be. Maybe it was noisy pipes, or perhaps they had active imaginations. Maybe one of the roommates was playing some kind of trick on everyone. I was trying to find a logical explanation for why everything was happening so that I could feel less fearful about going in and investigating, but something inside me was telling me that there was a lot more going on here than just noisy pipes.

When we got to Dean's house, I asked everyone to wait downstairs and asked Dean to walk up to the attic with me. I knew that once I opened up psychically, I would be able to feel everyone else's fears in addition to my own, so I decided the fewer people around, the better. As we were approaching the top of these very steep steps to the attic, I could psychically see an image of a male spirit dressed in black clothing, standing on the other side of the door. I felt so much fear, I didn't think I could go in there. The ghost appeared to have dark hair and almost black eyes. His face looked contorted with anger. I told Dean we needed to go downstairs and get everyone to come up with us. I no longer cared about feeling everyone's fear; I needed reinforcements!

As we were turning around to go back down the stairs, I could see the male spirit coming at me very fast. He floated right through the closed door and literally put his two hands on my back and pushed very hard. I threw my arm out a broken window, which just happened to be to my right, and was able to catch myself from falling. My heart was pounding so hard I thought it was going to come out of my chest. The total fear I had been feeling just moments before now changed to anger, and I was determined to do whatever I could to get this guy out of there.

We went downstairs and explained to everyone what had just happened. Everyone, including the skeptics, was anxious to go upstairs and see if they could see or sense this negative entity. We all headed up the stairs scared half out of our wits.

I told everyone that it was important not to show any fear and that if we got scared we were supposed to say the Lord's Prayer for protection, but I don't know if anyone heard me. No one else in our group had developed psychic abilities or had ever seen a ghost, but everyone was up for whatever was going to happen.

We got to the top of the stairs and everything was quiet. We opened up the attic door and nothing seemed unusual. There were several boxes piled high over to the right, and to the left there was a mattress on the floor with a little nightstand. Dean explained that someone actually lived up there, but apparently she had never seen or felt anything strange. He said she was kind of odd herself and thought maybe she just blended in with all the strange goings-on.

We decided to sit in a circle on the floor and hold hands. There was a light directly above our heads, which we decided to turn off. We just sat there on the floor waiting for something to happen. I began to see a very faint image of two forms standing over by the boxes. One was short, maybe only three-and a-half-feet tall. I found myself staring at that one because I was curious why it was so small. Then she came into view—a little girl about four years old. She was holding hands with the other form, which slowly took the shape of a woman.

They began to float toward us. Several members of our group reported that they could see them as well. All of a sudden from the left side of the room came the man dressed in black. The woman and little girl seemed really frightened and darted behind the boxes. Then he lunged toward our group. I knew everyone else saw him too, because several people gasped at once.

I quickly reminded the group to say the Lord's Prayer and not to show fear, but it was evidently too late because this man was getting bigger and bigger right before our eyes. He appeared about twelve feet tall and kept looming toward the group, obviously to scare us. I could see by the look on his face that he was thoroughly enjoying himself at our expense. Every time we got a grip and said the prayer, he would shrink in size. Amazing. Birdie had been right.

Finally I got up the courage to stand up to him. I yelled at him to back off and leave us alone. I told him that he had to leave Dean's house because they didn't want him there. He laughed at us and disappeared but then came right back. He did this several times, disappearing then coming back. Whenever he would disappear the woman and little girl would come out from behind the boxes, but they would never get too far before he would reappear.

I asked the woman and little girl why they were there, but they wouldn't answer me. The little girl was whimpering and rubbing her eyes. Her mother tried to console her but didn't seem to have much to give her. I was totally focused on the two of them when someone in the group hollered to me to look out. I whipped around, and this male spirit was right on top of me. He was so hateful-looking. I yelled at him once again to back off and leave us alone. I said that he was not welcome here and he had to leave NOW. We said the Lord's Prayer twice and it became very quiet. I no longer saw the mother and daughter, and the man seemed to have left. We sat for a few more minutes to see if this calmness was just temporary or if the ghosts had really gone.

After about five minutes with no more activity we decided to turn the lights back on, only to discover that the oddest thing had happened. There was a perfectly round puddle of liquid in the middle of our circle. We all kidded each other about who had wet their pants, but no one had, and none of us knew what this liquid was or how it had gotten there. There wasn't a leak in the roof. None of us had brought any water upstairs with us. There just wasn't a logical explanation.

Despite the unexplainable liquid, we felt pretty confident that we had done whatever needed to be done, and so we headed downstairs. We were still chatting about everything that had taken place when

I started hearing that whimpering sound again. I psychically looked around to see what was going on and, sure enough, there was the little girl. Then her mother.

I asked the mother what was going on, and she said she was really relieved that we had gotten rid of the guy because they were very frightened of him. She said that he had murdered them both then taken his own life and would not let any of them go on to the other side. She said they had been there for a long time. When I told her I didn't know what to do for her, she looked so discouraged and a few seconds later disappeared. That was the last I saw of any of them.

When we finally left Dean's house that night I was so glad to get out of there. I realized how exhausting this ghostbusting work is and hoped I wouldn't have to do it too often. Little did I know what was in store.

Facts About Ghosts

Ghosts can actually feel your fear; they can even breathe it in and grow larger from it. If you are in a fearful situation with a ghost, say a prayer (the Lord's Prayer, for example) that will help you feel at peace and protected. Always ask your guides to protect you. If you feel something close to your face taking your breath away, tell it to back off NOW. Remember, you are more powerful than any entity. When they are breathing in your breath or the energy from your fear, it's just an indication that they are not feeling very powerful and are trying to draw on your power.

Who Ya Gonna Call?

THROUGHOUT most of the 1970s I had my hands full working a full-time job during the day and doing my psychic work in the evening and on weekends. If memory serves me correctly, I didn't get any other calls about ghosts for quite a while. I'm not sure exactly how many years passed between my second encounter with a ghost and my next, but my guess would be about seven.

In the spring of 1980, I made a decision to quit my day job and work full-time as a psychic reader and spiritual healer. As with all new businesses, it took off slowly, and many times during those first few months I wondered if I had made a wrong choice by quitting my barbering business. By fall, I was pretty discouraged because the calls weren't coming in as I had hoped they would. I wasn't doing any advertising because my inner voice told me not to, so all business came by word of mouth. One day I sat down and asked God to please give me a sign as to what I should do, and the very next day, a reporter from our newspaper, the *Star and Tribune* called for a brief interview for a Halloween story they were doing. After talking with me for over an hour, the editor decided to do the feature story on me instead; within twenty-four hours, calls for psychic readings and healings started coming in from all over the country and my career took off.

I also started getting calls from people who suspected they had ghosts. By this time I had learned quite a bit more about ghosts and felt a lot more confident in my "ghostbusting" abilities, so when a call came in from a young woman named Martha who said she had moved out of her house because she believed it was overrun with ghosts, I decided to check it out. She said that the house had been on the market for over a year with no interested buyers, and she was sure the ghosts were responsible.

I was intrigued, if a little scared, by all the symptoms she described. Even though I was used to seeing spirits by then, they were usually the friendly type, like spirit guides. Ghosts are a whole different story. They usually have an attitude, and most of the time they aren't real friendly.

By this time my brother Michael was doing psychic readings for a career as well. When we were kids, we didn't get along very well because he was always so hyper and I needed a lot of calm around me, but as we got older our personalities seemed to complement each other and we got along really well. He's the comic in the family, I'm the "straight man." We often help each other cope with our psychic abilities, and I asked him if he would go to Martha's house with me to see if we could find any ghosts. It seemed as if it would be a fun thing to do together. It turned out to be quite an experience for both of us.

It was a Sunday evening. We pulled up in front of a small west St. Paul home, and on the outside everything looked so normal. A white picket fence surrounded a front yard, with hedges that had grown quite tall. The For Sale sign swung in the breeze. The house looked as if it had a fresh coat of white paint on it, and the awnings were trimmed in black. Looking at it from the outside, it seemed hard to believe that this sweet little home in the city could actually be overrun with ghosts. When we got to the door, Martha told us she had just arrived herself. She seemed a little on edge and told us that she hated coming here, hated the feelings she had while in the house and really hoped we could do something. She said she had spent hundreds of dollars on exterminators and other professionals, trying to find what was causing the problems, and she was at her wit's end. We sat down in the living room and she introduced us to a friend of hers whom she had brought along. Then we introduced her to Michael's wife, Katie, whom we had brought along. We explained to her that the first thing we wanted to do was walk through and get a feel for the place.

Before we go any further, let me explain something about these ghostbusting stories. I realize it's part of my job to create the scene for you so that you can see what I saw as I walked through each experience—describe to you what each room looked like, the pictures on the wall, the colors and textures of the furniture, the smells, all the minute details that create these scenes in your mind. The problem is that when we're looking for a ghost, we have to keep the lights down low, for one because it's easier to see ghosts in the dark, but also because our psychic eyes are scoping out the environment on a different dimension. Yes, our human eyes are open and aware of our physical surroundings, but our concentration is elsewhere. So that's where the problem comes in. I often can't remember any details about people's homes! If and when I can, I will certainly share them with you. Now back to Martha's.

Michael and I opened up psychically, and within seconds we saw our first batch of ghosts. Right in the living room there was a group of six spirits sitting around a table. They were holding hands, and it looked as if they were praying. We looked at each other, and Michael asked me if I could see the spirits sitting at the table. Yes, I told him, I could. They were very faint and it was hard to make out what they were doing at first, but they had their heads bowed and they were mumbling something.

I asked them what they were doing there, and one of the men said they were members of a prayer group that had met there every Sunday night when they were living and that they had continued to meet there on Sunday nights since dying. Besides feeling the presence of many other spirits in the house, we could also feel some pretty strong vibes coming from Martha's friend, who clearly thought we were con artists. Michael asked the woman to please wait in the living room while we walked through the house. Looking for ghosts is taxing enough without having to duck someone's negative vibes.

There was a small stairway over to the left of the living room that led to the upstairs bedroom, and we decided to begin there. Michael went up first, I followed right behind him and Katie was behind me. I don't know what prompted me to look behind me, but I turned around to look at Katie and right behind her was a male ghost with a very snarly, angry look on his face. He put his hands around her neck as if he were going to strangle her. I yelled at him to get away from her and he immediately disappeared. She told me she felt something really weird going on around her but had no idea what it was. Although Katie is very sensitive, she has not developed her psychic abilities. She came along with us that night just to see what might happen.

That experience sure freaked us out. Our nerves were starting to get a little raw. Next we spotted the spirits of two small children, a little boy of about five and a four-year-old girl. The little boy had dark hair, sunken-looking eyes, and a pale complexion, and he was dressed in a white shirt and dress pants. The hollowness in his eyes was so sad to see; it looked as if he'd been ill. So I wasn't surprised when, after we asked them what they were doing there, the little boy said he had been sick and then he died and that he came to this lady's house to play with her toys.

The little girl looked a lot healthier. My guess, just from her appearance, was that she didn't die from an illness but rather from some kind of accident. She had light-colored hair and was wearing a yellow dress. Her energy was very up. She told us that when she died she came here to play with the little boy so he wouldn't get lonely. They were playing some game and seemed oddly happy, although the energy around them seemed very lonely.

When Michael crouched down to their level to talk with them, they scurried off into the closet. Then I saw an image of a young male ghost, about sixteen years old, standing right next to Martha's bed.

He appeared in all leathers that were tattered and torn. He told me he had died in a motorcycle accident in front of this house several years before and had come inside the house rather than go to heaven, because he thought it was going to be really boring over there. He said he loved jumping up and down on Martha's bed and scaring her at night. It felt as if he was trying to impress me with how tough he was.

I was feeling pretty overwhelmed by all of the ghosts in this house. All I could think of was what we were going to do with all of them. I had no clue. I just knew there were more to find, and my energy was already running low. We decided to go down to the kitchen to regroup. We needed to take a little break because being wide open psychically, as you need to be when searching for a ghost, can be exhausting. Fortunately the kitchen was clear of any ghostly entities.

We were sitting at the table for less than a minute when we started to smell the strangest odor. We looked around the kitchen, half hoping not to find whatever was causing the weird stench. The smell led us to the bedroom right off the kitchen, and there on the bed lay a female ghost who actually looked like a skeleton. She was moaning and seemed delirious. Wow, it was so creepy I just wanted out of there. We tried to communicate with her but she was very incoherent. She just kept moaning. She gave off the strongest odor of death. Even Martha's friend the skeptic came in and asked us what the horrible smell was.

Right then and there we just wanted to quit ghosthunting, but we decided to keep going and get the job done. We headed for the basement, where we immediately saw a male and female spirit standing over by the washing machine talking. Michael asked them who they were and instantly they disappeared. We checked the rest of the basement and found nothing else, so we ventured back upstairs to tell Martha everything we'd found.

Turns out that everything we'd found coincided exactly with the experiences she'd been having. She said the only room people felt comfortable in was the living room. Sometimes she could hear children giggling in her closet, and some nights she could feel something sit or jump on her bed when she was trying to go to sleep. She said that wherever she went throughout the house it always felt as if there was a man watching her. She hated doing the laundry, because there was a spooky feeling by the washing machine. She said she absolutely hated going in the spare bedroom by the kitchen, because she could smell something really weird in there but could never find the source.

We talked for a while about how the ghosts had affected her life. She desperately needed someone to talk to who would understand what she was going through. With all the spirit experiences Michael and I had been through during our psychic development period, we understood completely.

After Martha seemed calmed down we went back upstairs to begin the process of getting the spirits to move on. We asked our spirit guides to please help us with each situation, and as always they were right there to help. When we started talking to the sixteen-year-old about going on to the other side, he again told us how boring he thought it would be and said he wanted to stay here.

Our guides suggested that we ask the young man if he would take the two children over to heaven. They felt that once the teenager got there, he would see just how wonderful it is and would undoubtedly choose to stay there. We called the children out from the closet and asked the young man if he would assist them to the light, which he agreed to do. He asked us if he could come back once he got them over there, and we told him of course he could (which he could), but we felt pretty confident that he wouldn't be back. And that's exactly how it went.

He took each one of the children by the hand and we talked them through the tunnel. They slowly moved toward the light, and as they moved we could feel all of them let go of their earthly existence. We burned some sage (more about this in the last chapter) to clear out all the fear energy in the room, and then went back downstairs. Martha then surprised us when she said that she didn't want us to get rid of the prayer group. She said they actually made her feel good, so we moved on to the spare bedroom. We again asked our guides for assistance because this old female soul was not paying any attention to us, and they suggested asking for an angel to come and take her on to the other side. They said we should explain to her where she was going and tell her that an angel was going to take her there.

Right after we finished explaining this to her, a beautiful female angel came into the room and scooped the woman into her arms. Within thirty seconds, the two of them were floating out of the room. We saw the angel carry her through the tunnel and into the light, which, I must say, was very cool to watch. Again we could feel that sense of release as one more of these earthbound souls let go of life on earth.

We ran downstairs to make sure that the man and woman had not come back and found the basement empty. We walked through the house one more time to make sure there were no more spirits hiding anywhere. We burned more sage and asked God to clear and bless this house. Four hours after we had first walked into Martha's house, we were done.

We were exhausted mentally, physically, and psychically. We each just wanted to go home, take a shower, wash all the vibes off us, and get a good night's sleep, which is exactly what we did, but only *after* stopping at a fast-food drive-through on our way home. Michael and I had worked up quite an appetite by this point and had had such an amazing experience that we had a lot to talk about. Working together was great, and it was very validating for both of us that we always saw the same things. We were learning so much about ghosts and how to get them over to the other side, which was really cool. We talked about how scared we felt at certain times and how at other times we didn't feel any fear. We could see that we could really be of some help to people, and that felt good.

About two weeks later we called Martha to see how everything was going. She said she had moved back into the house the next day and hadn't experienced any of the old ghost symptoms. She told us that the house had sold the following weekend and that she and her brother had gotten the price they had originally asked for. She was so happy, and so were we.

After Martha's house was cleared, word seemed to spread that we had the ability to get rid of ghosts, and we started getting calls from other people with haunted houses. Slowly we became known around Minneapolis and St. Paul as the brother/sister ghost-busting team. We started getting invitations to appear on different television and radio shows and were written about in lots of magazines and newspapers. We couldn't believe how our careers were taking off because of people's fascination with ghosts!

We've never counted or kept track of our clients, so I can only guesstimate that over the last twenty years we've gone into well over one hundred homes and dealt with hundreds of ghosts. Michael and I don't always work together, though we do when our schedules permit. Sometimes I take along one of my students who is interested in learning about ghost-busting, and once in a great while, I'll go by myself —if the job doesn't sound too scary!

My ghostbusting stories are as varied as the ghosts that they are about. It all boils down to being good at dealing with all sorts of people . . . these people just happen to be dead!

Facts About Ghosts

When there are children ghosts in a house, we've found it works very well to ask one of the adult ghosts, often the one most resistant, to escort the children to the light and through to the other side. We tell the children to hold hands so that none of them wanders off as they make their way through the tunnel.

CHAPTER FIVE

He Wanted the Kids Out of There

NOT ALL GHOSTS are here to make trouble, but once in a while we find one who's just downright mean. A young couple called and told us that their two small children, ages three and four, were complaining that there was a "mean man" in their bedroom who was trying to push them down the stairs. The mom said that she wasn't sure if there really was something there but that she was concerned because the children were afraid to be in their room and wouldn't stop talking about this man.

We decided it would be best to do this job when the children were asleep so as not to call any more attention to the situation. We went over to their home about 9:00 that night. We could tell immediately that this couple was nervous about our being there. The woman kept apologizing for asking us to come over, and the man told us he didn't think there was anything there. He just thought the kids had overactive imaginations. As we explained to them how we did our work, we were both psychically scanning the house for any indication of earthbound spirits. There was definitely a *feeling* of a ghost somewhere, listening to our conversation. It was just one of those feelings when *you know* something's up, and we were anxious to find out what it was. First we checked out the living room and dining room. No ghosts. The husband's home office had a lot of tense energy in it, but it too was clear of ghosts. But when we got to the kitchen, it started to feel creepy. I didn't like it at all. We could feel angry male vibes in there, and we could tell they weren't the vibes of anyone who physically lived in the house. They felt old and stale, which usually indicates that there's a ghost somewhere around the area.

We began to head up the stairs to the bedrooms, and I suddenly felt gripped with fear. I could see a presence slowing beginning to form at the top of the stairs. I told Michael I didn't think I could go up there because it was really creeping me out. He told me to wait in the kitchen. He said he would bring the ghost downstairs because he wanted to talk with him without waking up the kids.

I stood at the bottom of the stairs and watched him walk to the top of the stairs and begin talking to the ghost. He asked him what his name was, and the ghost answered, "Roy." Michael asked Roy why he was here in this home, and Roy told him he liked this house—well, actually he liked the adults but hated the kids and just wanted them out of there. He said that he had tried several times to push them down the stairs but it wasn't working, and that he really liked scaring them. Then, when Michael told him we had come to get him to go on to the other side, I could feel Roy becoming very angry.

Then something happened that I had never seen before. The hallway filled up with a very thick, gray energy, almost like a fog. It was so thick that I couldn't see my brother. I called to him and asked him if he was all right. His voice was very soft, but he told me not to worry. I kept telling him to talk to me, tell me what was going on, but for several min-utes—probably four or five in all—he said nothing. My guides told me to stay downstairs, that this ghost was just filled with hatred and that I didn't need to feel it. They reassured me that Michael was okay, although I had my doubts. My big fear was that this Roy had entered Michael's body and that was why he wasn't answering. But just as I was about to go up-stairs and get him, I heard Michael tell Roy to go downstairs because he wanted to talk to him away from the children.

When they got down to the kitchen, I was sur-prised to see how fragile Roy appeared. He was a little under six feet tall, with light brown hair, and eyes that were shrunken in. He had this really awful gray aura and looked very thin, almost like skin and bones (strange way to describe a ghost, I know, but he had that malnourished look, which, believe it or not, not all ghosts share).

I asked him why he hadn't gone on to the other side, and he said that his parents had been very abusive to him when he was living and that he didn't want to go anywhere where they might be. He was so adamant about it, I didn't think we were ever going to get him to go over to the light. We asked our guides for some help, and they came up with a brilliant suggestion. They told us that when Roy was alive he had had a dog named Copper whose soul now resided on the other side. They said they would go get Copper and bring him to this room, and that we should tell Roy that if he wanted to be with Copper he would have to go over to the other side with him. They also said to reassure him that he would not have to come in contact with his parents.

They left the room to get the dog, and Michael asked Roy if he had had a dog when he was living. Yes, he said, he had had a golden retriever named Copper. Right about then the dog's soul came leaping into the room, and Roy was down on the ground hugging and kissing him. The dog was as excited to see him as he was to see the dog.

We told Roy that if he wanted to hang out with

Copper he would have to go on to the other side, because that is where the dog resided. We both reassured him that he would not have to see his parents. We told him to just tell the greeters on the other side that he did not want to see his parents, and it would be all right. We could see that he was really struggling with the decision; he hated his parents with a passion, but his love of Copper convinced him to go.

We watched as the two of them floated through the tunnel and into the light. What an incredible experience. We both knew that animals have souls and go on to the other side, but we had never had an animal be a part of a ghostbusting job.

We went back into the living room and told the young couple what we had found. We reassured them that the ghost was gone. Before leaving, we burned some sage and walked through the house one more time, asking that it be cleared of all negative vibes and blessed. We advised the couple not to say much to the children other than that the man was now gone and they were safe. We also warned them not to talk about the ghost while in the house, for the next three days, because we had learned the hard way that if people talk a lot about their ghost, right after a ghostbusting, the ghost can hear them from the other side and sometimes get the impression that he is missed. In some cases, the ghost has actually returned.

After we left, we sat in the van for at least five minutes and just stared out the window. I asked Michael what he was doing upstairs in that gray hazy energy, and he explained that he just sat there so he could feel Roy's energy and what it felt like to be Roy. He said it was a cold, dead nothingness, and he was real glad to be done with the job. As usual, we headed for a fast-food restaurant before going home. We cranked up the radio to get us grounded back here on earth and chatted about everything under the sun *but ghosts*.

Facts About Ghosts

Children and animals can see ghosts and spirits easily. Their intellect isn't getting in the way, telling them it's not possible. If your dog growls or your cat hisses at nothing, or your children talk to "nothing," chances are you have a ghost or a visiting spirit.

CHAPTER SIX

He Was Afraid God Was Mad at Him

IN MY psychic development classes, our teacher taught us that all suicide victims go to a place in between our plane and the other side, called limbo, where they remain until the natural time of their death would have occurred. When we went on this next ghostbusting job, I was glad to find out that that information did not apply to all souls who commit suicide.

My mom got a call from a treatment center in Minneapolis that had formerly been a funeral parlor. They were doing a lot of reconstruction on the building, and the workers were complaining about a certain part of the building that was giving them the willies. Some very strange noises were apparently

coming from an old elevator shaft that had been
boarded up for years. Workers also complained that
their tools were being moved around and said they
felt as if something or someone was watching them.

Mom asked Michael and me if we would go check
it out because the owners were friends of hers and
she was concerned about them. When we first
arrived, we did our usual walk-through, just to see
what we could find. There were definitely a lot of
spirits floating around the place. There were three in
particular who appeared out of nowhere and came
looming at us really fast, as if to purposely try to
scare us. I must admit they had my heart pounding
for a few minutes. I'm used to ghosts trying to hide
from us, not looming at us. Turns out they were
teenage ghosts, all dressed in black leather clothes.
They were quite obnoxious. They yelled and laughed
and generally tried to scare us out of there.

We saw ghosts hiding behind plants and others
roaming the halls. We made our way up to the third
floor, and that's when we came upon the boarded-up
elevator shaft. Psychically, Michael and I could both
see the soul of a young man who appeared to be
hanging. We looked at each other, wanting confir-
mation from the other that we were both seeing this.
We walked closer to the elevator and asked the young
man what his name was, how old he was, and why
he was there.

He told us his name was John and that he had hanged himself at the age of twenty-one. He appeared to be quite emotional, as if he were crying. We asked him why he didn't go on to the other side, and he said he was afraid to go to heaven because he was afraid God was mad at him for taking his own life. I asked my guides about the whole idea of him going to limbo, and they said that that information wasn't accurate. Suicide victims could go into heaven like everyone else, they said, but a lot of times they don't feel worthy of going because they have taken their own lives, so they just find someplace here and stay stuck.

We told the young man he could go into heaven, and he said he didn't believe us, so we asked our guides if they had any suggestions as to how to help him. They suggested that they go to the other side and bring his parents (both deceased) to this place. They said maybe the parents could convince him to go home with them. We asked our guides if they would please find them for us, at which point they left the room. It was about thirty seconds later that our guides and John's parents came floating into the area. They floated right up to John and the three of them hugged. It was quite an emotional scene. They told John that God wasn't angry with him for taking his own life and that he had suffered enough in this elevator shaft. They said he was welcome to come home with them. They told him about other relatives who were anxious to see him again. He looked at us and asked if all of this was for real, and we told him, yes, it was. He was quite anguished about whether or not he was doing the right thing, but after a few minutes of thinking it all over, he left with his parents and we watched them all float into the white light.

We both felt so good about what had just happened that it made the rest of the job go a lot easier. We made our way through the rest of the treatment center and cleared out the remaining twelve ghosts.

Facts About Ghosts

Many times we have found a ghost so filled with remorse, guilt or shame about something it did during its lifetime that it is completely stuck. It won't allow itself to go on. Deceased loved ones do come and try to get these ghosts to come home with them, but many feel they must stay here in a "state of limbo" and be punished. The truth is, they are the ones who condemn themselves to limbo, but they can set themselves free whenever they're ready to.

CHAPTER SEVEN

The Ghost Was in Love

ABOUT ten years ago I received a call from a real-tor who said that a house he was trying to sell had been on the market for several months and all the prospective buyers seemed frightened before they even got in the front door. Some would turn around and leave without going inside. Michael wasn't able to go this time, so I took along my good friend, Mike Warnell.

As we walked through the house I couldn't see anything, but I could feel someone watching me from the third floor. As I approached the master bed-room on the third floor, I could feel an angry, cold energy standing around the corner. I had chills all over my body.

I walked into the bedroom and there he was: a male ghost standing on the side of the bed where the woman of the house slept. In my dialogue with the ghost, he told me that his name was Bob and that he was in love with the woman who lived there. He didn't want her to move! I had already discovered that ghosts don't usually move with people when they move out of a house, because they tend not to like (or are frightened of) change. To keep his beloved from moving out, Bob had taken to standing by the front door to frighten anyone who came to see the house.

Ghosts can become as obsessed with people as people can, and this ghost named Bob thought he was very much in love with this woman. The woman then told me that she had had a couple of dreams about some man who was interested in her. In one dream, her wedding ring was removed and put on top of the bookshelf. When she woke up the next morning, she found that her ring was off. Because the shelf was so high, she had to get a chair to stand on in order to see if the ring was on the top shelf. There was no way this woman could have done all of that in her sleep.

My guides directed me to have the woman tell Bob that she loved her husband and wanted Bob to leave her alone and go to the other side NOW. She did this and then I talked to Bob about letting go and moving through the tunnel. He said he was lonely and wanted to be in love. I reassured him that he could find a relationship on the other side. He seemed relieved and said he was willing to give it a try. I directed him to look for the light and move toward it, which he did. After seeing him go into the light, I saged the house from top to bottom to get rid of all the negative energy in there.

Before leaving, I reminded the homeowners not to talk about Bob for a few days, while in the house, lest he think he was missed and come back. I called about a week later to see how everything was going, and they had already sold the house. They asked if I would go check out their new house to make sure Bob hadn't gone over there. I did go, and he hadn't. He remained on the other side.

Facts About Ghosts

Ghosts can be romantics, too. Sometimes a ghost gets really attached to someone on this side and can't let go. If you think a ghost may be smitten with you, be very direct and tell it to move on. If you're serious and it can sense it, it will move on.

CHAPTER EIGHT

"I Don't Want to See My Sister"

A GOOD FRIEND of mine and I were driving up around northern Minnesota one fall day, just going from town to town exploring the area via the back roads. At some point, from the road, we could see the top of an old house back in the woods and decided to go investigate. The dirt road that led to the house was almost grown over with weeds. As we drove up closer, I could see a faint image of an older woman ghost standing in the window on the second floor. She was just standing there looking out the window as if she were in a trance, just a blank stare on her face. She noticed that I was watching her and ducked back from the window. My friend stopped the car and suggested we go inside. I'm usually pretty chicken about things like this—I'm the one who worries that the sheriff will pull up and arrest me for trespassing. But I decided to take a risk and go check out the ghost.

The front door was wide open, so we walked right in. The place was filthy. There was fifties-era wallpaper on the walls that was half torn down, old broken-down furniture, and torn curtains in some of the windows. Lots of cigarette butts all over the floor. Big holes in the wooden floors. I could feel the presence of young people in the building, as if it was a hangout for teenagers. I wanted to get out of there because it smelled so bad, but I kept feeling pulled upstairs. I wanted to find out if there really was an older woman spirit standing near the window.

I didn't mention anything about the ghost to my friend, just in case I was imagining it. A part of me was hoping she wasn't there because I wasn't in the mood for ghosts. I wanted to play, not work, but I felt an obligation to at least see if there was a stuck soul upstairs. I told my friend we needed to check out the upstairs, and he just rolled his eyes.

Up we went and there she was, standing in a bedroom all by herself. She looked to be about eighty-five years old, white-haired and frail. I slowly approached her and asked her what her name was and why she was here in this old abandoned house. She didn't give me her name but told me she used to live nearby and that when she died she decided she did not want to go to heaven, because she didn't want to see her sister. She said her sister had always been terribly mean to her when they were living and that she had been so relieved when her sister had died. Then, when she herself died, she didn't know what to do to avoid her sister, so she decided to take refuge here. She said the house she used to live in no longer existed, so she found this one and stayed.

I asked her if she knew what year it was, and she didn't have a clue. I asked her if she could remember what year she died. Nope, couldn't remember. She told me she had never married.

I asked her if there were other deceased members of her family, but she just stared out the broken window again, as if she were back in a trance. I told her I thought she should move on into the light and start a new life for herself. She looked at me with a blank stare. Then she asked me two questions that I had never been asked by a ghost: Could she wear pink in heaven, and could she get her hair done there? I told her I didn't see why not.

Then she asked what she should do about her sister. I told her heaven was a big place and that there would be angels that would help her over to the other side if she wanted their help, and all she needed to do was tell them she did not want to see her sister. Again she asked whether she could get her hair done there, and again I told her I didn't think it would be a problem. She agreed to go.

I asked my guides if they would ask an angel to come and help her over to the other side, which they did. I talked her through the tunnel, even though the angel was with her. I could sense that she needed the reassurance. It took about five minutes total but she did go into the light.

Later on I asked my guides if they had directed us to that old house, and they just smiled.

Facts About Ghosts

There are lots of stuck souls here who simply do not want to go on to the other side and face certain people from their lifetime. It's much better to do what you can before dying in the way of forgiveness and amends so that you don't end up a soul hiding out on earth.

CHAPTER NINE

A Policeman Named Bill

ONE NOVEMBER, on a rainy Sunday afternoon, I got a call from a very frantic young woman who said she was the owner of a massage parlor in Minneapolis and that some very strange things were happening there. She said they were experiencing banging on the walls and could feel someone watching them. She told me that there had been an incident the night before where *something* had ripped the shower curtain off the rod when one of their "johns" was taking a shower. The man had grabbed his clothes and run out of there. I told her I would come check it out that night.

When I got there I found a lounge area, where I met two of the masseuses. They were very nice young women who were obviously frightened by the events taking place in this building. I could see into several massage rooms, each softly lit, with a massage table and some oil. On this particular evening there were no customers, so I just roamed the halls looking for the ghost. Was I ever surprised to round one corner and come face to face with a male ghost dressed in a policeman's uniform. He told me his name was Bill and that he had died three years earlier near the parlor. I asked him if he knew about the tunnel and the white light and he said that, yes, he was familiar with both. He said that several of his deceased relatives had come to try to convince him to come over to the other side, but that for now he chose to remain on this side and protect the girls.

He said when he bangs on the walls, it's a sign to the girls that they need to beware of this particular patron because he's not safe. Then he asked me to tell the owner that he was sorry about ripping the shower curtain off the rod last night, but that he'd really lost his temper when he realized that the john in the shower was a priest. When I told her what he'd said, she was convinced that I'd seen her ghost. How else would I have known about the priest?

Through me, Bill asked if he could please stay and continue to protect the girls. He said the banging on the wall was not to frighten them but to protect them. The owner had joined us by this time. The girls took a vote and unanimously decided to keep him. Bill reassured me that when he was ready to move on, he would go into the light.

Facts About Ghosts

Souls will sometimes stick around if they're older and genuinely concerned for people on this side, or younger but using that as an excuse. We can always tell if the concern is genuine or not, but in either case, we reassure the ghost that there are many people on this side who can help these people out. The ghost needs to learn to let go and trust that people will take care of themselves or find others to help them.

CHAPTER TEN

The Ghosts Were Stoned

ONE DAY Michael and I were called to the home of a young woman who was terrified to sleep in her bedroom. She said she could feel something watching her every night. She had wanted to call us for some time, but her landlord didn't want her to. He said he didn't believe in ghosts and thought we were just scam artists. After many discussions about this, the landlord agreed to let her hire us to do her room only, but we were to leave the rest of the house alone.

It was a beautiful home in the wealthier part of Minneapolis. Built in the early 1900s, it had all the original woodwork, elegant staircases, big stone fireplaces, original chandeliers. At first it was fun to walk through this very regal-looking home, but once we opened up psychically we saw a whole different picture. The place was crawling with ghosts, and there was something very odd about them. We didn't know what was going on at first, so we just kept moving through the house. We met the landlord, who seemed like a nice guy. Although outwardly he acted as if he believed in what we did, we could feel his skepticism. As we sat in the kitchen talking with him, the oddest thing happened. We started seeing spirits go in and out of him. At first I thought I was seeing things, but when I asked Michael about it, he said he saw it too. We kept watching to get a better understanding of what was going on, and then one of my guides told me that this man smoked a lot of pot and that the spirits would go in and out of him throughout the day to get high. Now it made sense to us that he didn't want us to do any of the other rooms. He was being heavily influenced by these drugged spirits and wanted to be left alone.

When we were finally alone with our client again, we asked her if the landlord smoked pot, and she said, "Oh yeah, all day." We asked her if his personality changed much, and she said, "All the time." At that point there weren't too many spirits in her room, but there was definitely a feeling that these spirits did not respect people's boundaries and would probably wander into her room whenever they felt like it.

We did a general ghostbusting. We told all the spirits that were in her room to leave and to stay out. We heavily saged the room and then we visualized sealing the room in a white light, which, according to our guides, sets up an outer boundary so spirits know not to come in. It was hard for both of us to leave that day, knowing that the landlord was being possessed regularly and that the house was filled with stoned ghosts, but we had to respect his wishes. It did not feel right to say anything to him about what we had observed. This was how he liked living his life.

I talked to the client a couple of weeks later, and she reported that the difference between her room and the rest of the house was so significant she was thinking of moving out. She said she really liked the energy in her room, which had remained clear, and wanted to go find a place to live that had that feeling all throughout.

Facts About Ghosts

Souls who had a drug or alcohol problem when they were living may choose to hang out with people who have a similar addiction and may actually take over their bodies from time to time in order to still feel that high. If you are an alcoholic or drug addict, ask God or your spirit guides to protect your body from these entities, especially when you're intoxicated.

CHAPTER ELEVEN

She Was Bouncing Him Off the Walls

EVERY TIME I think I've learned everything there is to know about ghosts, I get a call that leaves me speechless. In the summer of 1991, we received a call from a woman who rented out several rooms in her house to men. She said that some very unbelievable things were going on in her house. One of her renters, Tom, a man well over six feet tall, was being attacked by a ghost every once in a while. She was afraid to tell him that she'd called us, because she was afraid he would get mad, but we asked her to please have him there when we arrived so we could ask him some questions and make sure this was for real.

We had some difficulty setting this up. Every time we made an appointment with them, they canceled it. Finally the third appointment was a go. Our client asked her renter to be at our meeting at 6:00 P.M. At 7:15 he came strolling through the front door with a real attitude. He wouldn't even look at us. Strangely, until he got there we hadn't seen any ghost activity at all, but within minutes of his arrival Michael and I both saw a female ghost standing down the hall by Tom's room. She was standing around the corner thinking we couldn't see her.

Slowly Tom began to tell us what was going on. He said there was a female spirit around the house who had a crush on him. Whenever he brought a woman home to his room, the female spirit would become really jealous and start slapping him in the face. According to him there were a few times when she picked him up and threw him into the walls. Here's this six-foot-three-inch man looking at me, telling me that this female ghost picks him up and throws him into the walls when he brings a woman home. I'm sure my mouth was hanging wide open. I looked at my brother for an explanation, but he looked as perplexed as I felt.

Turns out the man was really upset with his land-lady for interfering. He liked this ghost. He told us he thought it was kind of cute the way she threw him around and that he wanted to keep her. He told his landlady that if she insisted on having us get rid of the ghost, he would move out. It seemed very clear that these two people needed to figure out what they wanted to do. We told them to call us if they decided together to get rid of the ghost, because if we tried to do it at the landlady's request, Tom could always call his ghost friend back from the light. We never heard from them again.

Facts About Ghosts

Some people think of their ghosts as pets, and what's sad is that these souls often think of themselves as pets. They're grateful to be loved, no matter how it comes. When we run into this type of situation, we talk to the ghost about going to the other side and developing some real relationships with other souls. We tell it that it deserves better than to be someone's pet. These ghosts usually have very little self-esteem, so we are gentle and loving toward them. But it is also important to be firm about the fact that they need to set themselves free and begin a new way of having relationships. Ghosts are people, not pets.

CHAPTER TWELVE

He Didn't Know
He Was Dead

THIS WAS ONE of those jobs that completely took me by surprise. Up to this point, all the ghosts I had encountered knew they were dead, but this young man seemed to have no idea. One chilly fall evening in 1986, I was called to a house near the University of Minnesota campus. A young woman had called saying that something was knocking books off book-shelves and jumping up and down on her bed. Also, things were being moved from room to room. Clothes had been thrown out of the closet and onto the floor. She said she was afraid to come home every day for fear of what would happen next.

When I walked into her bedroom, I immediately saw the ghost of a young man in an army uniform with blood all over the front of it. I asked him what his name was and why he was there. He said his name was Kenneth and he was there to get his house back. He said he had come back from Vietnam and this woman was living in *his house*. I asked him what year he thought it was. He said 1968. He told me he'd done everything he could to get this b——h out of his house, but that she wouldn't go. I asked him if he knew he was dead, and he argued that if he was dead I wouldn't be talking to him.

He went into a rage, yelling at me to get out of the house and leave him alone. "Take this b——h with you, too," he said. My first reaction was to yell back, but I decided instead to approach him gently and to talk to him calmly about his situation. He obviously needed help accepting his death. It looked as though he had died in Vietnam. His memory was very fuzzy. All he remembered was going off to war and then being back here in Minneapolis, trying to get back into his house.

When I told him he needed to accept that his physical body had died, he appeared to start crying. (Yes, souls do release their emotions through crying, but their tears aren't wet!). He told me he didn't want to be dead, that he was only twenty years old. He alternated between being really angry and really upset. He must have told me at least a half dozen times that he wasn't dead and to get the hell out of his house. We went around and around about why he should have to go on and why I didn't make *her* leave instead. Sometimes he would disappear and then reappear again.

It was a long two and a half hours before something shifted and Kenneth became willing to go through the tunnel to the other side. I just kept telling him he deserved to be free. He was young and could make a fresh start for himself. I asked him if he could remember family members or friends from Nam who had passed away. He said that he remembered a couple of buddies who had died in the war. I told him he could see them again if he went over, and that seemed to bring some comfort to him. Reluctantly, Kenneth moved into the tunnel and toward the white light. He thanked me as he moved to the other side.

I instructed the young woman who lived in the house not to talk about him for a few days, because he would be able to hear her and might get the impression she wanted him back.

Three days later, I got a phone call from the woman's roommate, telling me Kenneth was back. The roommate told me that the woman had really missed Kenneth and asked him to come back. He told me that if things got really crazy again, he was going to move out. I never heard from either of them again. I guess this young woman realized that she would rather live *with* Kenneth than without him. I guess we'll never know what happened to the roommate.

Facts About Ghosts

Sometimes if a person doesn't believe in life after death, he will not move on to the other side when he dies, because he won't understand what's going on. He will simply hang out in a place most familiar to him here on earth. Sometimes when loved ones from the other side come to these people's aid, they think they're just hallucinating. The good news is, most people do believe in some kind of afterlife, so this doesn't happen that often.

When you're dealing with souls who don't believe they're dead, it's important to be honest and direct and tell them that their physical body is dead and that there is a very special place for them to go. We tell them to look for the light, and we strongly encourage them to move toward it. We tell them that their deceased loved ones are in this special place and that they will be reunited with them as soon as they get there. We repeat this several times so that they really get it that we're not some kind of hallucination, and that this is all for real.

CHAPTER THIRTEEN

His Kids Were Afraid to Sleep Over

WITHIN an hour after getting a call from a producer at NBC's *The Other Side*, wanting to know if I had any interesting ghostbusting jobs, I got a call from a man in South Minneapolis who was really upset because his children were afraid to sleep at his house. He explained that his nine-year-old daughter Samantha was complaining of a creepy feeling in the house, and his fourteen-year-old son Daniel was seeing and hearing spirits in the house. Daniel could apparently hear children spirits playing in the attic, bouncing a ball and laughing, and could also see an angry male soul roaming the halls of their beautiful home. The final straw for the dad was the day he ran out to his car to get something, and when he got back to the house something or someone had locked the front door from the inside. But no one was home but him!

I asked him if he would be willing to be on TV, and he said he was open to doing whatever he had to so that his kids would be comfortable staying over again. It turned out to be a really fun show to do. The camera crew was great, and Dr. Will, the show's host at the time, came to Minneapolis and slept in Daniel's haunted bedroom. The show hired a sketch artist, Paul Johnson, and also invited Dale Kaczmarek, the president of the Ghost Research Society, to join us with all of his electronic equipment that measures ghost activity.

The attic was quite different than I'd expected. It had been completely renovated and was really beautiful—white carpeting, all new windows, walls painted white, skylights in the ceiling. A regulation pool table sat in the middle. There was a big-screen TV off to the side, with a beautiful leather couch across from it. The father told me he had had the attic completely redone, hoping his kids would enjoy coming over, and he was angry that the ghosts were interfering with their lives.

As I walked around the attic, I could see six children ghosts on the other side of the billiard table, sitting in a circle playing with a ball. Ghosts can create the same kinds of things we have here, simply by thinking of them. They are invisible to us because they are not made of matter, but they are visible to the ghosts—and to me. If children ghosts want to play with a ball, they simply think of one and they have one.

I walked over and sat down on the floor, so as to be right at their level, and asked them who they were and why they were there. One by one, they gave me their names, first names only: Annie spoke first, then Dougy, Timmy, Susy, Connie, and Marky. Annie said they all lived in a house over there and pointed in a direction west of the house. I asked her if they were related to each other, and she said no, that they were not related, but had all lived together, gotten sick and died around the same time. I asked her why they didn't go on to the other side, and she said they didn't want to, they just wanted to play. They didn't want to grow up.

One by one, each child drifted out of the house. I asked Annie where they were going, and she said that they played at other houses in the neighborhood too. I asked her if they would all come back later, and she said yes, they would. Just as she was leaving, she told me to watch out for the mean guy who lived downstairs. I wasn't sure if she was talking about the owner or a spirit, but it seemed as if she was talking about a spirit. When I shared all this with the owner of the house, he nodded, saying he'd been told there used to be an orphanage just down the road which had burned down.

Once all the children were out of the attic, we moved downstairs to look for the angry spirit that Daniel spoke about. I found him sitting in the TV room off to the side of the living room. He was about six feet tall, with dark hair and eyes, and he had a scowl on his face. I asked him what his name was and why he was there. He said his name was Roger and that this was his house. I asked him if he had been a previous owner of the home, and he said that he could never have afforded this house, but that now that he was dead, he had moved in and taken over. He talked about how lonely he was and told me he enjoyed scaring the little kids in the attic. Then he moved out of the room and disappeared.

I walked through the rest of the house—all four floors of it—and in a closet in the basement found a ghost named Elmer. He seemed very disoriented and spoke somewhat incoherently about his wife, Rose, wondering where she was. It seemed as if maybe he had Alzheimer's or something. He was very confused about his existence. I asked my guides for help, and they said they would go get Rose but that I needed to talk to Elmer and help him understand that he was dead. My guides went and got her from the other side. It was one of those sweet reunions where all it took was getting them back together to get the stuck one to move to the other side.

My guides told me that Rose had been there to get him before, but he didn't understand what was going on and wouldn't leave with her. Once I could see that the two of them were in the light, we moved back upstairs to try to find Roger again. He was sitting over on the piano bench in the front room.

I showed Dale Kaczmarek where Roger was sitting, and he put one of his "ghost meters" on top of the piano. It definitely registered ghost activity. This gadget had ten lights on it; depending on how much ghost energy there was in the room, a different number of lights would light up. This time I think about six lights lit up. We were all quite impressed.

I asked my guides what to do with Roger because he was such a crabby guy. They suggested that Daniel be the one to tell Roger to go on to the other side. Daniel could see him and had seen him roaming the halls of this big house many times. Roger liked scaring Daniel. It just seemed right for all concerned that Daniel be the one to tell Roger that he was not welcome and that he needed to move on to the other side. Roger asked me if it was possible to find a relationship on the other side, and I told him yes, definitely! That got his attention. Both Daniel and I urged him to move through the tunnel into the light, and after arguing with us for a while about why he shouldn't have to go, he finally did leave.

It was now around 11:00 and we were all getting tired. We had been at this for hours. When you do a TV show like this, you have to set up the camera equipment and all the lighting in the room you are going to shoot the scene in, and then move it all to the next room. It can take many hours just to film an hour's worth of film. We had been at it since about 3:00 that afternoon. We still needed to go back up to the attic and see if we could pick up any ghost activity on Dale's equipment from the children.

When we got there, all six of them were up there playing with their ball. They were cute all right, but they looked so drawn, so blank in their eyes, as if there was very little life in their little souls. I had no idea how long it had been since they'd died, and they didn't seem to know either.

Dale set up his equipment on the floor near the area where I showed him the children were playing. One by one the children came over to see what was going on. As the children got close to the machine, the lights on the meter went up to five or six. We put a real ball on the floor and the producer had me ask the children if they would move the ball. They tried, but to no avail. It's just not that easy, especially with energy as low as theirs was. They tried several times to get the ball to move, but it just wasn't happening. Their little hands kept going right through it.

I asked the children to gather around because I wanted to talk to them about going away. I told them that going to the other side didn't mean they had to grow up. I said that there was a lot to do over there and a lot of toys and fun things to play with. I encouraged them to take each other's hands and move into the tunnel and toward the light.

Dougy seemed to be the most mature, so I asked him if he would be the leader and take them over. He was so sweet and said yes, he would do that. They all held hands and I coaxed them through the tunnel. I kept telling them they were doing a good job and to just keep going. Finally they were at the light. I told them not to be afraid, that they were going to be very happy there. I urged Dougy to just keep going, right through that light, which is exactly what they did. What a rewarding day.

For those of you wondering how Dr. Will's night in the haunted bedroom went, the next morning he reported that he'd slept like a baby!

Facts About Ghosts

Oftentimes it's better that the owner or resident of a house tell the ghost to leave and go toward the light, first because it's empowering to the resident to know he can make this happen, and also because it gives the message loud and clear to the ghost that it is not wanted.

CHAPTER FOURTEEN

The Log Cabin
in the Woods

IT WAS IN the summertime of 1993. I had taken time off from ghostbusting for a few months because I had grown weary of arguing with souls who wanted to stay stuck. My brother's life was going in one direction, raising his two children, and mine was going in another—I was teaching classes three nights a week and seeing four clients a day for healings. As full as my plate was, when I got a call from the TV show *Sightings*, wanting to know if I would fly to Colorado Springs and identify some ghosts for a segment they were doing on hauntings, I couldn't resist. I always learned so much from the ghost stories that the TV shows came up with, and they were just fun to do.

They said the only problem was that these ghosts

only came out at night, and they wondered if I'd mind working from midnight to morning. Sounded intriguing. I was scheduled to teach two workshops the same day they wanted me to fly out, but there was no other time we could all do it, so I decided to just look at it as an adventure. It had been a while since I'd been up all night!

It was a very hot day in mid-July. I did the two workshops, raced home, took a shower and headed for the airport at about 6:00 that night. I arrived in Denver around 10:30. We were held up in the air for a while because there was a violent thunderstorm going on. It was pretty eerie—lightning all throughout the sky, rain pouring down. I remember thinking how perfect the weather was for filming a spooky segment for television, with all that thunder and lightning crashing in the background.

Scott, the owner of the haunted log cabin, was at the airport to pick me up. He was very open about not believing in ghosts. He said he didn't know what it was that had taken over his house, but that he certainly didn't believe in disembodied spirits. He was from Louisiana and had a strong southern drawl. As we drove through several towns in Colorado, with the thunderstorm pounding outside of the car, I listened to him tell me story after story about some of the things that went on in his house: beams of light coming through the house, UFO sightings near his property, police confiscating photographs he showed them and then claiming they had never seen them. He said that he and his wife Bev would lie in bed at night and watch a light show of different colors on the ceiling. They would hear chains rattling around in their house. At times they heard voices, other times footsteps. Things would move from room to room. He and his wife had decided to install sur-veillance cameras inside their house to take pictures of all the activity.

It took close to an hour to get to their house up in the mountains. It was a big, beautiful, rustic log cabin. A fog hung about ten feet above the ground. There were no streetlights or stars to light the pitch-black sky.

When I entered the three-story log cabin I was quickly greeted by the producer, who asked if I would mind having a seat while the scientist they had hired told us about his ThermaCam. It was a very expensive camera that was used to measure intensities of heat in a room, thereby possibly pick-ing up ghost activity because a ghost has a coldness to it and that would be detected by the camera. I was more than glad to just sit and relax for a while. It was close to midnight and I was starting to get a little tired.

No sooner had I sat down than a voice behind me said, "Hey, hey, over here." I turned around, and to my right there was a male ghost. He seemed to be about six feet tall, wearing blue jeans and a blue-checked flannel shirt. He smiled at me, and I sent a thought back to him to please be quiet because I wanted to hear what the scientist was saying. Well, he didn't care, because he just kept saying, "Hey, hey, look over here." Then I heard it in unison. I turned around again, and now there were five male spirits, all dressed alike, except that each one had a different-colored flannel shirt on.

The original ghost said his name was Tom and told me that this was his house, that *no one* was going to make him go to the other side. He ran the show around here and had for a long time. I hurriedly told the producer what was happening just in case he wanted to get our dialogue on tape, which he did. The producer set me up with a microphone, and the conversation began. Tom told us why he and the boys felt they deserved to stay in the house. This was his land, his home, and he was not willing to leave it. He said he was a lot like Scott, the new owner. He talked about Scott and Bev for a while and gave me quite an earful on the history of the area.

The cameraman, to whom I had not yet been introduced, asked me if these guys were responsible for knocking his very expensive equipment off the countertop. All five ghosts answered with a resounding "*Yes*" and then disappeared completely out of sight. Meanwhile, the scientist, Ted, had turned on his ThermaCam, and we did record on film the change in temperature in exactly the same spot where Tom had stood.

We decided to walk through the house to see what else I might find.

There in the living room over by the big picture window were three more male spirits. They looked as if they had all just come in from a fishing trip. None of them would talk. They just stared at each other. I tried two or three times to get a conversation going, but to no avail. They just didn't want to talk. Two or three minutes later, they disappeared.

The producer asked Bev if she would show me some of the photographs of the ghosts they had taken over the years. He was curious to see my reaction. We sat at the kitchen table, and just as we started looking through the photo albums, some dogs outside started barking. It was somewhere between 1:00 and 2:00 in the morning, so it seemed strange that anyone would be outside, but the dogs would not stop barking.

In order to be able to pick up sound on the microphones, the camera crew needed to quiet the dogs down, so the producer went outside to see what was wrong. When he opened up the door, a huge, ten-foot white mass of energy came into the house. Of course no one could see it but me. A voice within this white mass told me that "they" lived in the forest and that they didn't come into the house very often, but they were curious to see what all the commotion was about. They had seen lights set up around the out-side of the house (the crew had put them there to create a scary effect) and the vans and cars parked outside, so I guess it was reasonable that they would wonder what was going on. I told the producer about the white haze, and Bev asked me if it looked any-thing like this one photo that had been taken by their surveillance camera.

She showed me the photo, and yep, it was exactly the same. Actually, I was in awe of this beautiful white energy. I explained to the voice within the mass that this was a television crew, taping a seg-ment for a TV show. He simply said, "Oh, okay," and out of the log cabin the white mass went. Bev then told me that when she put this particular picture on the computer screen she could see actual faces in the haze.

Suddenly the energy around Bev and me changed. Now there were three different male spir-its standing right by us. One had a particularly mean scowl on his face. He started touching us then walked through us, at which point Bev and I jumped about three feet off the ground. His energy was so cold. He came right up to my face and tried to take my breath away, which ghosts will do sometimes in order to become bigger and more powerful. Earth-bound spirits can come right up to your face and take your breath as you're exhaling. It's a very suffocating feeling, as if you can't get enough air. My teacher taught us to tell the spirit to back off and leave us alone when they do something like this, but you need to sound *very* firm.

The good news is, I could see him, so I told him to back off and leave us alone. I asked what his name was and what he wanted. He said his name was Raymond. He would back off for a minute or so and then come right back at both of us. He kept trying to bug us by touching us. At one point, he put one hand on my back and one hand on Bev's back at the same time, and again, she and I jumped up about three feet yelling at him to leave us alone.

Earlier, Scott had told me that he had had to take time off from work because he had come down with chronic fatigue syndrome. I'm certain that Raymond was responsible for it, sucking Scott's energy out of him daily. He seemed like such a taker, a leech. He kept coming at me, trying to get energy from me, and at one point, I could feel myself getting drained. My teacher had told me to be very firm when dealing with ghosts like this and to tell them to back off. This was not the time to get wimpy or start believing that the ghost had more power than me, so I told him to back off and leave me *alone* now! He did leave the house, but I suspect he probably came back the next day after we all left.

By this time, it was almost 3:30 in the morning. We were all getting pretty tired, so Bev brought out a bunch of food she had prepared for us. Pizza, turkey, chips—you name it, she had it. We decided to lighten up a bit and *not* talk about ghosts for a while, so we shut off the cameras and microphones and took a break. No sooner had I made a sandwich than one of Bev's friends, who was sitting at the top of the basement stairs, started hyperventilating, shaking and crying. She kept saying "Get it out of me, get it out of me." It completely took me by surprise.

I looked inside her to see if any of the spirits had jumped into her, but saw nothing there. Bev was trying to calm her down. The producer was hollering for me to do something. The cameraman was trying to get his equipment set up to get all of this drama on film. My spirit guides were telling me to go into a room by myself because they wanted to talk to me. I yelled back to the producer that I would be there in a second, but that first I had to find out what was wrong.

The guides told me to get her into a chair in the kitchen area, because that was where the energy was positive and clear, the room where we were all laughing and *not* telling ghost stories! They said to burn some sage and surround her in smoke. I was to put my hand on her back and Bev's hand on her chest and have her say several times, out loud, "I am clear, I am clear." She was convinced there was a spirit in her, but, the spirits assured me, there wasn't. They said she was very sensitive and that her body was acting like a psychic sponge, soaking up all the negative energy in the house. They said she should not be here and that as soon as we got her calmed down and cleared, we should get her to go home.

It took a good solid five to ten minutes, reassuring her over and over that she was not filled with a negative entity, and her continually affirming out loud that she was clear—body, mind, and soul— before she finally settled down. Shaky but clearheaded, one of their other friends drove her home. My guides had me tell her to go home and go right to bed, not to sit up and rehash what had happened. We didn't hear from her after she left, so I assume she was okay.

By now it was close to 4:30. We were sitting waiting for the crew to set up their equipment in Scott and Bev's bedroom, a room where most of the ghost activity seemed to be. Another one of Scott's friends came over to visit and handed me a visitor's brochure of the area. He said it talked about the original settlers of the area and a guy named Tom, who had been the sheriff back in the 1800s. It sent chills up my spine because I knew that this was the same Tom I had met several hours earlier.

One more room and we were done. We were all exhausted. The cameraman and audiowoman were husband and wife. They were a great team, really fun to work with. They had to deal with a lot of frustration that night. First their very expensive camera was knocked off the shelf, and all throughout the night the audio equipment had a high-pitched sound to it. The only time it would stop was when I was having a dialogue with the ghosts. We all surmised that somehow the ghosts were creating the sound and that they were quiet only when they wanted everyone to hear what they had to say.

We walked into Scott and Bev's bedroom, and there, sitting in a rocking chair in the corner, was Bev's deceased grandmother. Over to the right of the chair was the closet, and there was Tom and his four buddies. There on their bed lay two male ghosts, and there was another one standing in the corner. No wonder they felt so much activity in their bedroom— the banging on the walls, the footsteps, the lights on the ceiling, voices, a feeling of someone watching them. They had told me earlier what a hard time they had sleeping in there. *No kidding!* This is where all the ghosts congregated. I couldn't imagine trying to get any sleep in there.

I went around to each ghost and asked it what it

was doing there. Some of them wouldn't talk to me. Tom and his buddies would move in and out of the room. Grandma just liked being there. We were all so tired that I decided to just burn some sage and tell them to clear out. I was concerned about leaving some of them there, so I asked the spirits to *please* leave these people alone and go on to the other side. They left the building, but I don't believe they went on to the other side.

I did not do an official ghostbusting on each ghost because the producer had only wanted me to identify the ghosts, and besides, everyone just wanted to get some sleep. At about 6:00 in the morning, after heavily saging the house to get rid of any negative energy such as the fear and anger, we packed up our equipment and headed back to our hotel.

I have spoken with Scott and Bev a number of times since our original meeting, and they say the activity has continued. In case you're wondering if Scott ever became a believer, he said he's going to remain on the skeptical side until he has more proof.

There's a line in the movie *The Sixth Sense* about ghosts only believing what they want to believe, and I would have to say that's just as true of many of the living. Ghosts really do exist, whether we choose to believe in them or not!

Facts About Ghosts

The more fuss that's made about a ghost, the more ghosts you'll attract. Portals are openings from our world into the spirit world. The most common way to create one of these portals is by working the Ouija board, because it's inviting communication. The problem with opening ourselves up to the spirit world without knowing what we're doing is that we attract all kinds of souls to us that may not be so favorable. If you suspect you have a portal in your home, ask the universe to close it up, and read up on psychic protection. This is nothing to mess with.

CHAPTER FIFTEEN

Bobby Mackey's Music World

IN OCTOBER 1991, *Sightings* called to see if I would fly down to Wilder, Kentucky, and check out a bar called Bobby Mackey's Music World. The associate producer told me she didn't want to tell me anything about this place because she was curious to see what I would find. She said I did not have to get rid of the ghosts, just identify them. It certainly had my curiosity going. I figured if they were willing to fly me all the way to Kentucky for a day, something must be up.

The day before I left, I came down with a strange cough, and by the next day, I barely had a voice. I wasn't sure if I should go down to Kentucky or not, but decided that once I got there I would probably be all right. On the plane I got concerned about how psychic I would be since my energy was so low, so I asked God to please help me feel more confident and give me some energy to do a good job. I arrived in Cincinnati about 2:00 that afternoon and took a cab across the river to the bar in Kentucky. The cab driver asked me what I was doing in town, and with some hesitation I told him I was a psychic and was sent to this bar to see if I could find any ghosts.

I barely got the whole sentence out of my mouth when he asked me to give him a reading on his career. I asked him what his first name was and immediately started getting psychic information on him. His career, goals, relationship, it all just started flowing. It was exactly what I needed in order for me to know I was on track psychically. When I arrived at the bar, the producer of the show was waiting outside for me. He quickly opened the door, helped me out of the cab, and thanked the cab driver. I looked at the driver apologetically, as if to say, "Sorry I can't help you with more," and he was sitting there with his mouth wide open. The only thing he said was that he had never had such an experience in his life and that everything was amazingly accurate. Good, I thought. I said a quick prayer of thanks to God and moved on to the next thing, which was this bar.

The building was over one hundred years old. It was wooden, with brown paint that was chipping off everywhere. It had no windows, and it was tilting to the side. It gave off a very thick negative energy, which a lot of old bars do. There were railroad tracks in the back and a river running nearby. It was cold outside, the leaves were off the trees and it just looked so old and desolate, as if it could easily fall apart in a strong wind. As I was standing there looking at this scary-looking building, the producer explained to me that they wanted me to walk through by myself.

Normally the camera crew is walking about six feet ahead of me in order to catch my reactions on film, but in this particular situation they wanted me to walk through first with just a microphone on. The lighting inside was very poor, and in order to get good shots, they had to do quite extensive setup for each shot.

The producer said they would give me the floor plans if that would make it easier for me. The more I looked at this place, the more creeped out I got. I finally interrupted this man in my raspy-sounding voice and asked him if he would please walk through with me. I didn't feel that I had the energy to do this all by myself. There was something so creepy about this place, and I kept thinking, something must not be too cool in there if they were willing to fly me down here. The good news was that he was willing to go with me.

They put a microphone on me, and I began the walk through. First stop was the women's bathroom. No ghosts in there. Next was the men's room. There, standing behind one of the stalls, was a male ghost wearing cowboy boots and a cowboy hat. He startled me by smiling and saying, "Howdy ma'am." I said howdy back and giggled as I walked out. I figured this wasn't the bad ghost I should be searching for.

We moved on to the large bar area, and there I found three male ghosts arguing at a table. I walked over to them and asked them what they were arguing about. They told me they loved to drink and get into fights. They said that they would wait until guys were drunk in the bar and then they would enter their bodies and start fights. They were very immature souls, real rowdy. Just wanted to party and fight. I kept on walking. There was a male ghost behind the bar playing bartender. There was a female ghost standing up on stage singing a song. The bartender ghost told me she stood there all day singing songs. Hmmm. Other than the three bullies, none of these ghosts seemed to be a problem.

I told the producer I needed a couple of minutes just to get my bearings. I stood apart from everyone and psychically scanned the building. I could feel an energy down in the basement and asked the producer if we could go downstairs. They decided to go ahead and set up the camera equipment, so I sat for a few minutes and took a break. There were several people there that day watching us tape. So far I had not been introduced to anyone. They wanted my psychic impressions first.

As soon as they had everything set up, they came back upstairs and got me. In order to get to the basement we had to go down a very steep set of stairs on the outside of the building. As the producer opened the door, I was looking at the stairs and just told myself to go slow and I would be okay, when out of the blue, something came up from behind me, put hands on my back and pushed really hard. I screamed and grabbed onto the railing. I turned around, expecting a person to be standing there. I saw a female ghost. I yelled at her and asked her why she had done that.

She was so shocked that I could see her that she bolted around the corner and disappeared. I asked the producer, who was now standing at the bottom of the stairs waiting for me, if one of the bad ghosts was a female that pushed people down the stairs. He told me he was impressed but would explain later because now we had to get to the basement while the lighting was ideal.

This basement was one of the creepiest places I had ever seen. It reeked of mold and mildew. Each room I passed seemed creepier than the last. There was junk everywhere, as if pack rats had saved things for years and years. I could hear moaning, people talking in a different language, cows mooing and weird chanting going on somewhere, but I couldn't find the source. Some of the rooms I just couldn't stay in. The vibes were hard to describe, other than very negative. There was such a feeling of death down there. Then I came upon a room that had two ghosts in it—a female and a male. The female was sitting down. She had her hands on her chin as if she were holding her head on her neck, and she kept saying, "Oh my head, oh my head." The male ghost was pacing back and forth and kept saying to her, "It's all your fault we're here, it's all your fault we're here."

I told the producer what I'd found, and he became very excited. He asked if there was anyone else or if I could describe them. I could feel another male on the other side of the wall, so I walked to the next room and there was a male ghost about six feet tall or under, with dark eyes, dark hair and a thick dark mustache. He was quite agitated. I asked him if he knew the two people in the other room, and he said yes, and began pacing himself. I asked what his name was, and he said Scott. I walked back into the other room and asked the ghosts in there what their names were. The male said something that started with an A, but I couldn't make it out. His eyes had a vacant stare to them and seemed so cold-blooded. The woman would not answer me. All she kept talking about was her head. That was all the information I could get from them, except that when I asked them how long they had been here, they said something like the late eighteen hundreds. I found it hard to believe that these three characters might be the reason for the trip. They all seemed pretty harmless.

The producer seemed very happy with the work that I had done and told everyone to take a break and meet back upstairs in ten minutes. He wanted me to meet with the scientist they had flown in and one of the owners of the bar, Janet Mackey.

I went upstairs. My energy was getting drained by all the spirit activity. All I wanted was to get out of this damp, dark bar and breath some fresh air. I walked over to the bar to get a drink of water, and the ghost bartender asked me if he could get me anything, which got me laughing. I told him I would get it myself, but thanks anyway. Then he disappeared. I sat there drinking my water, hoping nothing would interrupt my break. I glanced over at a folder on the bar and there was a picture of the two men I had just seen down in the basement! I think I let out a yelp, I was so blown away. I had never seen actual photographs of ghosts from when they were still living! The captions identified them as Scott and Alonzo. There was also a picture of a woman named Pearl. Whoa, this was exciting. This was the woman I'd seen in the basement, too! I took the photos and ran over to the producer and told him that these were the three folks I'd seen down in the basement. He said it was time we all had a meeting.

I sat down with Janet Mackey, Dr. Roland (not his real name), Carl (the caretaker) and the producer, and I told them everything I had found. Janet explained all the things she had experienced in the bar: being pushed down the stairs when she was five and a half months pregnant and going into premature labor, seeing a headless woman walking around the bar, hearing voices telling her to get out of there, the jukebox playing the "Anniversary Waltz" when it was unplugged, employees complaining of being pushed, the male bartender ghost behind the bar, a dark-haired ghost with a handlebar mustache. How eerie to hear her talk about some of the very things I had just seen!

Dr. Roland asked me to direct him to where I thought there was the most ghost activity. He wanted to set up his equipment there. I told him to go to the last two rooms on the right side of the basement, and he would find them there. He said he'd call up to me by walkie-talkie when he had everything ready to go. About fifteen minutes later, he called upstairs and told me that he had his instruments set up in the two rooms but nothing was registering. He asked me to come downstairs.

I hated the thought of going back down those stairs but was curious to see what his equipment did, so, watching very closely for the female spirit at the stairs, I went back down. No sign of her. When I got to the rooms, I found all three ghosts right where I had last seen them. Dr. Roland had his computer set up right in the middle of the room. This computer supposedly measured ghost energy. If there was a ghost present, the bells in his computer were supposed to go off, but nothing was happening.

I asked my guides what I should do, and they said to take this equipment and put it inside Scott's "stomach area," which would then register on the computer. I asked the doctor if it was possible for me to move his equipment, and he told me to be careful but go ahead. I walked over to Scott and asked him if he would mind if I put this gadget inside his stomach. He said he didn't mind. As soon as I did, the bells on Dr. Roland's computer went off like clockwork!

We went into the next room, where Alonzo and Pearl were, and did the same with them. The computer rang out with these two also, although not as strongly. I asked the doctor if we could take the computer to the female ghost at the top of the stairs, which we did, and the bells went off with her too. Pretty exciting stuff.

We all went back to the bar, and they proceeded to tell me the story of the ghosts in Bobby Mackey's bar. It's quite a story, and it's all collected in a book by Doug Hensley called *Hell's Gate*. If this story is of interest to you, I recommend getting Doug's book. He did a ton of research on this famous bar and it's all in there.

The building was originally built in the early 1800s and was a slaughterhouse. In 1802 satanic worship rituals went on there. Later on, the Cleveland mob owned and ran it as a nightclub for many years. One of the nightclub singers, a guy named Robert Randall, got the owner's daughter, Johanna, pregnant, and the owner killed him. Johanna then poisoned her father and jumped to her death. I think someone told me she was five and a half months pregnant at the time. The club was shut down for some time after that.

Then around 1896, either Scott Jackson or Alonzo Walling was dating a woman named Pearl Bryan. Pearl became pregnant and announced that she was going to tell the townspeople who had gotten her pregnant if he didn't come forward and take care of her. One of these two men chopped off her head and buried it somewhere near the bar. The two men were then hanged at the gallows in 1897, both claiming they hadn't done it. Alonzo said he knew of the crime but didn't do it; he said he'd come back to haunt this place forever after.

Patrons and employees of the bar have always said that when they smell the scent of roses in the bar they know someone is about to die, and it has happened every time. Johanna wore rose-scented perfume. I asked my guides if Johanna was the woman who tried pushing me down the stairs, and they said yes, that was her. I asked them why the three in the basement didn't go on to the other side, and they said:

A. That the men were afraid if they went on to the other side, they would be sent to hell for killing Pearl.

B. Pearl was still in love with Alonzo and was hoping they could work things out.

C. She felt her due punishment for getting pregnant was to have her head chopped off, yet she had a tremendous amount of anger towards both men and had decided to hang out and make their "lives" miserable.

D. Pearl could set herself free from this little triangle anytime, but so far she had chosen to stay in it. She wanted Alonzo to acknowledge his relationship to her, and until he did, she was going to stay there.

Wow. This whole thing had happened so fast, and before I knew it, it was time to leave for the airport. Once again, the media were making these ghosts out to be evil monsters, but they're not. There wasn't anything evil going on here. The bar was just filled with a bunch of stuck souls. I didn't help get rid of them (once again I was only hired to find them), but I was hoping they'd eventually move on.

• • •

Six years later, in June 1997, I got a phone call from a television show called *The Unexplained.* They wanted to know if I had done any really interesting stories in the last few years. I told them about Bobby Mackey's place. I had already been on several other shows, talking about this case. The *Sally Jesse Raphael Show* flew several of us to New York to talk about it on the show. Geraldo did a show on it, too.

The producer of *The Unexplained* called the bar to see if any more activity was going on. When they heard that it was, they called and asked me if I would be interested in doing a follow-up. I said sure. I was very curious to see if the gang was still there. I also asked the producer if we might have some extra time so that I could do a ghostbusting and send any of them to the light who wanted to go. He said we would make the time.

About three weeks later, the day I was to leave for Kentucky, I developed the strangest cough. I didn't give it much thought until the morning when I got up to go to the bar. I realized I barely had a voice. Déjà vu. This seemed pretty eerie to me. I had to take two different cabs because the drivers didn't know where I was going. I had laryngitis so bad that neither one of them could understand me, and they didn't know where the bar was. After getting two completely different sets of directions from people on the street, we finally found the bar. I felt as if I was in the Twilight Zone.

I walked in and nothing had changed! It was as if time had stood still. Some of the same faces were still there (living people, that is). The bar looked and smelled the same, except that this time it wasn't a fall day; it was 91 degrees outside and about 100 degrees inside. One of the bouncers told me that a ghost had been getting in fights with people and he felt sure it was Alonzo. He also said that something or someone had hit him on the back of the head with a beer bottle, sending him to the hospital. This man is no small weakling, so it was hard to imagine.

I began my walk-through just like last time. Women's bathroom was clear. The cowboy was no longer in the men's bathroom, but Alonzo was! I was very surprised to see him upstairs. He started talking right away and asked me if I could help him get out of there. He said he hated it there. He was tired of people talking about him. He said it was like living in hell and he had to get out of there. He couldn't take it anymore.

When I told him that I'd help him go to the other side, he wasn't sure what I was talking about. He just knew he wanted to get out of there. He pointed to a woman halfway down the bar and said I should talk to Johanna and see if she wanted to leave, too. When I asked him about Scott and Pearl, he didn't say much, which gave me the impression that maybe they weren't speaking to each other.

There were several male ghosts sitting up at the bar pretending that they had beer glasses in their hands and that they were drinking from them. The male bartender was still there, but his energy was very weak. I could barely see him. I approached Johanna, and right away she apologized to me for trying to push me down the stairs. I was very surprised that she remembered me, and she said that there weren't that many visitors who could actually see them, so that's why she remembered me.

She told me she was very tired of this existence and that she wanted to leave. Was there anyplace else besides this bar to live? It was as if she had been there so long, she couldn't remember any other existence. Her energy was also very weak. She didn't have the anger that she had had six years before. She was worn out. Ready to move on. I told her I was going to send Alonzo on to the other side and that she should think about whether or not she wanted to go with him. I told her I needed to continue walking through the bar and that I would be back to talk to her. She told me to watch out for Gregory, and she motioned over by the pool room. I asked her who Gregory was, and she said he was the guy that was starting all the fights. She said Alonzo wouldn't do that and that people had it all wrong. She said this Gregory was a really mean guy. Hmmm.

I cautiously walked over to the pool room area, where I found a male ghost standing up against the wall. He was dressed in blue jeans and a dark blue shirt. He had on cowboy boots and told me he usually wore a cowboy hat, but didn't have it on today. I asked him if he was Gregory, and he said to call him ". . . Buck, Buck, Buck. Call me Buck." I asked him why he was there, and he told me he was a close personal friend of Bobby Mackey's. He said he killed a man with his bare hands. We chatted for a while. He was one angry ghost.

At one point in the conversation, he seemed to get tired. He told me he would be right back, and I saw him go over to the other side of the bar. I could tell he was going to suck the energy out of someone, and I thought he was headed for the bouncer, but he took energy from the female bartender instead. When I went over to the bar to see how they were feeling, she was sound asleep and the bouncer was slowly losing his energy. This Buck was not a good ghost. Another leech like Raymond.

I have very little patience for ghosts like this, so I left him and went downstairs to find Pearl and Scott. There they were, still in the last room. Their energy was also very weak. I tried convincing them to go into the light with Alonzo and Johanna, but they wouldn't even consider it. They were afraid to go on to the other side, for fear of being sent to hell. I told Scott he had spent enough time in hell already just living in this basement, but he just would not budge. He and Pearl were staying. After about ten minutes I gave up and went back upstairs.

Meanwhile, the producer had asked the bouncer to call Bobby at home and ask him if he had had any close personal friends, now deceased, named Buck, so when we got back upstairs, the producer gave me four names and wanted me to tell him which Buck this was. The first name he gave me felt like the Buck that I had just spoken to, and, as it turned out, that was the Buck whose name Bobby had given them. Bobby didn't actually know if this guy was alive or dead but said that he was the black sheep of the town that he'd grown up in. He was a real mean guy who had killed his own brother, but Bobby didn't know what had ever happened to him. The producer said he'd check with the town records to see if there was a Gregory or Buck with the last name that we got, but I never heard how it all turned out. I can tell you that Alonzo and Johanna did move on into the tunnel and go over to the other side.

Here's how it happened: Before I left, I went back to the men's bathroom where Alonzo was still hanging out, and I asked him to get Johanna. Within seconds they both floated over to me, and I talked to them about moving away from this bar and looking for the tunnel. They held hands and went into the tunnel together. I told them to head right for the light, which they did. They'd both been physically dead for so long, they didn't have a lot of energy. What a relief to see them out of this bar and into the light.

Afterwards, I burned a lot of sage and walked through the entire bar asking God to please clear out all of the negative vibes in there. I warned the bouncer not to let Buck steal his energy and told him that it was important that he ask God for protection, because he seemed so vulnerable to these spirits.

All in all, it was a pretty successful trip. I had a terrible case of laryngitis that lasted for almost a week after I got back, but it was well worth it for me to see those two ghosts from the 1800s get free.

Facts About Ghosts

Ghosts and spirits in general have no concept of time. They can remain in the same room or area for years and years, never giving any thought to how long they've been dead or how much life is changing around them. They are literally stuck at a point in time in their consciousness. Honesty is the best way to handle a situation like this. We tell the ghost, "This is the year 2000; it's important for you to move to the light."

CHAPTER SIXTEEN

The Spirit Kept Entering His Body

EVERY YEAR around Halloween we'd hear from someone in the media who wanted to do a piece on ghosts. One year, the television show *Encounters* called and asked if we had any interesting ghost stories. I told them we didn't have anything right then but that I'd call as soon as I got something. It's always so amazing to me how these so-called coincidences work. By the end of the day, we got a call from a woman who thought she had ghosts.

She said she was very frightened to stay in her home and could feel something watching her. She was afraid to go down to the basement because three cats had mysteriously died down there. She and her boyfriend—I will call them Kelly and Dick—heard banging on the walls and windows. Doors would open on their own. When they lay in bed at night they could hear music coming up the vents. Kelly told us Dick's behavior would get really strange from time to time. Although he was normally a very mild-mannered, almost timid man, one time he tried to strangle her in the middle of the night. Other times he would kick and scream at her. She said one time she found him unconscious at the bottom of the stairs. An ambulance took him to the hospital, and the hospital put him in restraints because he had gone berserk. When Dick woke up, he had no recollection of why he was unconscious at the bottom of the stairs or why he would have been put in restraints.

I called the show, and they were very interested in doing a story on this.

When we got to Kelly and Dick's house, we walked through it and found the ghost, Joe, right away. What an angry ghost he was. We first discovered him in their bedroom. The camera crew got all set up. We were going to talk to Joe and find out what his story was, but as soon as we were ready to talk to him, he disappeared down through the floor to the laundry room, the room Kelly hated to go into.

Michael ran downstairs to talk to him. The camera crew went down with him. Once again, as soon as everything was set up to begin shooting, Joe disappeared up through the floor, and there I was, face to face with this very angry ghost. Fortunately the camera crew had walkie-talkies, so Michael and I used those to talk to each other. This ghost was all over the place. He did not want to be pinned down or talked to.

Dick became very uptight with all the activity in the house. He told us he needed to sit outside and get away from the crowd. At first it didn't seem odd, because Dick was very shy and it just seemed reasonable that he would want to be off by himself. The problem, though, was that as soon as Dick went outside, we could not find Joe anywhere. It was just so eerie. Paul Johnson, the forensic sketch artist, sat Michael and me down at the kitchen table to make a composite sketch of Joe. He had each of us pick out Joe's features—eyebrows, eyes, nose, cheeks, lips, nose, chin, ears and hair—from several cards he had with him. We both picked out the exact same feature each time. We'd never done this before, so it was kind of fun for us to know that we really do see the same things.

After we were done with the sketch, we continued to walk through the house looking for Joe, but were having no luck at all. The producer was getting impatient and told us to make Joe come out now, because we had to get the show on the road. We realized the producer had no concept of what was going on here. He wanted to get the show "in the can," as they say, but you can't make a ghost do anything. We explained to him that Joe had disappeared and it was just a matter of waiting because we knew he would be back. Suddenly it dawned on me that maybe, just maybe, Joe had gone inside of Dick. I called to my brother, who had gone downstairs to look for Joe, on the walkie-talkie and asked him what he thought of the idea, and he called back to say his guides agreed that that was exactly what had happened. Joe had gone into Dick, as he had done on several occasions. That was why Dick couldn't be around any of us, because we would've been able to see Joe *in Dick's eyes.*

Michael's guides went on to say that years ago this fellow Joe had accidentally overdosed on drugs, trying to get his girlfriend's attention. He told her he was going to kill himself, she called his bluff, and he accidentally overdosed. The guides said Kelly reminded Joe of his old girlfriend, and that is why he tried to strangle her when he was inside Dick's body. We asked how he came to this house, and they said he used to buy his drugs from one of the former owners of the house before Kelly bought it. What a story!

We explained all of this to the producer and he really perked up. He wanted the crew to set up the lighting and their cameras before I told Dick what was going on, because they wanted to get his reaction on camera. I felt bad for Dick. I wouldn't want someone explaining something like that to me with a bunch of cameras in my face. As soon as everything was set up, the producer went outside and asked Dick to come into the house. Dick was reluctant to come in. He sat staring at us for a few seconds, almost as if he was trying to figure out how to get out of there. I think it was actually Joe who was hesitating because he knew that we knew. Dick finally did come into the kitchen and I explained to him that Joe was inside of him, possessing his body and that we wanted to channel a healing to him and pull Joe out of him. Dick was very willing to do whatever he had to, to get rid of this spirit once and for all.

Michael stood behind Dick, put his hands on his shoulders and began channeling healing energy to him, while I stood in front of Dick and started pulling Joe out of Dick's chest. Dick could feel the entity coming out. Dick was moaning and his body was jerking as I pulled Joe's soul out. They got it all on camera.

As soon as Joe was out of Dick, I continued to channel a healing to him, while Michael talked with Joe about the importance of getting on with his life by going to the other side. After about twenty minutes, Joe did go. I continued to fill Dick's body up with healing energy while Michael saged the entire house. We had Kelly walk through the entire house, and she said it felt completely different.

Three weeks later Kelly called to say Joe was back. Something felt very odd about the whole thing and I couldn't put my finger on it. I asked my guides what we should do, and they said this time it was up to Dick to stand up to Joe and tell him to get out of him. They said that Joe had entered Dick again because Dick had a problem with recognizing his own power. He saw Joe as more powerful than himself, and this was one of Dick's life lessons. He had to start standing up for himself. They said that if he didn't stand up to Joe, he would continue to be plagued by his presence or other spirits like him.

When I explained to Dick how to do this, what he needed to say and all, he was quite hesitant about the whole thing. He said a couple of times that he didn't think he could do it. My guides told me again that it was important that Dick do this, not me or Michael. We didn't hear from them again, but some mutual friends told me that Kelly and Dick split up, Dick moved out, and Kelly had a new boyfriend. I hope for Dick's sake that he stood up to Joe and set both men free.

Facts About Ghosts

Ghosts can be very self-serving. They do what they want, without consideration of what it's doing to others. Don't ever let a ghost "have its way with you," no matter what that means. If you suspect that you're being taken over by a ghost, do not under any circumstances put up with it. They need to honor boundaries just like the rest of us!

CHAPTER SEVENTEEN

How to Get Rid of a Ghost

BEFORE I go into the steps you can take to get rid of a ghost, I would like to share a newspaper article with you that one of my students gave me. Her great-aunt sent it to her back in the sixties from a newspaper somewhere around Chicago. In some ways, we've come a long way in our understanding of ghosts, and in other ways, I think many people today still believe this ancient folklore:

Sure-Fire Remedies to Rout an Uninvited Ghost

HALLOWEEN, traditionally the time for ghosties and ghouls and pesky things that go bump in the night, is just around the corner. Should you encounter any such phenomena and wish to be speedily delivered from them, we offer the following suggestions culled from ancient folklore. Sorry, but we can make no guarantees.

- If bothered by a witch, throw salt on her; it burns like fire.

- If a ghost crosses your path turn around three times and spit. Then address the specter in Latin. That will confuse the ghost and he or she will hurry out of the neighborhood.

- Worried about ghostly visitations while you're asleep? Hang a flour sifter at the foot of your bed before nodding off. Any ghost wandering in will see the sifter and feel compelled to start counting the holes. By the time he's finished, it'll be dawn and the ghost will have to leave before he's had a chance to do any mischief.

- Scatter black pepper around your bed; it keeps ghosts away. And last but not least, to repel ghosts—and probably anyone else for that matter—eat three garlic bulbs.

This article does remind me of a ghostbusting job Michael and I went on a few years ago. We got a call from some students in their early twenties who said they were part of the parapsychology department at one of our local colleges and that they had been called to investigate a haunted house in St. Paul.

They had been told by some experts to pour flour all over the floor and that when the ghosts came in, they would leave flour prints wherever they went. They also had pots and pans hanging from the ceilings, for the ghosts to make noise with, and a net, in hopes of catching one, but nothing was happening and they wanted us to come and check it out.

They did have ghosts, but the ghosts were all upstairs. They weren't interested in walking through flour, playing with pots and pans, or being caught in a net. Remember, these are souls with some intelligence. They know what's going on. If they see flour all over the floor and leave flour prints, it's because they want to make a mess, not because they don't know any better.

How to Get Rid of a Ghost

As you've seen from these stories, I can actually see and hear spirits, but you do not need these abilities in order to rid your house of unwanted guests. In order to succeed at ghost cleansing, there are two things you should always remember:

1. Your ghosts are unwelcomed visitors in your home. Don't treat them like all-powerful beings from the world beyond, who might get their feelings hurt if you confront them. They are not your friends or pets. They are stuck and need to move on.

2. Being invisible does not make them powerful. They are not more powerful than you. But it is important not to look or act afraid when you con-

front your ghosts. Be firm when talking to them about leaving. Remember, they are souls, made of energy. *You* are the one with the body.

Step-by-Step Instructions on How to Get Rid of a Ghost.

1. Go to the room where you feel the spirit's presence the most strongly or where most of the activity occurs. If it doesn't frighten you, walk around the room and feel for a cold spot. (This indicates where the ghost is.)

2. Tell the ghost out loud that he needs to turn and go toward the white light. Tell him he is not welcome in your home and you want him to leave now. Tell him to look for angels who will assist him through the tunnel to the white light.

3. At this point, you can ask for angels or deceased loving friends or relatives of this ghost to please come and assist him as he moves forward into the light. Wait for at least one or two minutes while friends and relatives gather around the ghost. While you are waiting, tell the ghost it is very important that he leave this plane of existence and get on with his life on the other side. As deceased friends and relatives gather, they will tell the ghost what to expect on the other side, thus calming the ghost's fears.

Often when this reunion takes place, the ghost becomes quite emotional, so you might want to lighten up your demands a bit. At this point in the ghostbusting, we usually become pretty gentle with the ghost and reassure him that he is making the right choice in leaving and going to the other side. Tell him you want him to follow his friends or relatives into the tunnel *now*. Tell him it is time to leave this place and get on with his life.

You will feel a slow, subtle difference in the room as the soul begins to let go and moves more and more into the light. Don't worry about whether or not you can feel it. It will be happening whether you sense it immediately or not. The ghost is leaving.

4. Open at least one window so that the sage and negative energy can exit. Next, take some sage, not much more than a quarter of a cup, and put it loosely in either an abalone shell or in a clean ashtray. Light it in three or four places and blow out the fire. Continue to blow on it. You want the smoke of the sage. Walk around the room, blowing on the smoke, or use a feather, fanning the smoke gently out into the room. Don't blow too hard, though, because you don't want sparks flying and you also don't want to set off the smoke detectors. You may want to disconnect the smoke

detectors while saging the room. Be sure to hook them back up when you're done.

While you are saging, ask God or the universe to please clear out all the negativity in the room. This will clear out the ghost's negative vibes and your negative vibes about the ghost, such as fear or anger.

For those of you wondering if you can use a smudge stick, yes, you can. A smudge stick often has two or three different herbs in it, such as lavender, fir or cedar. Sage is known for taking the negativity out. Fir, cedar and lavender are known for bringing good vibes or blessings into the room. We used smudge sticks when we first began, but my guides told us sage was quicker, and when you're doing a house that could have anywhere from one to ten to twenty ghosts, you want to do it quickly!

When you have saged the first room, you may want to go on and sage all the other rooms in your house. Oftentimes when people have a ghost, they have a lot of fear, and those fear vibes can linger in a house just like the smell of cigarette smoke.

As a matter of fact, I recommend saging your house periodically, just to keep it clear, especially after you've had an argument with someone or something traumatic has happened in the house. Sage will clear out the leftover vibes, so you won't think about the incident every time you walk into the room.

5. When you have finished saging the entire house, ask God or the angels to please seal your house from top to bottom with a white protective light so that no more intruders will come into your home. This step is very important.

6. We have found that if you talk about your ghost a lot after getting rid of him, he sometimes thinks you want him back, so he comes back through the tunnel, and all of the activity starts over again. If you want to talk to someone about this experience, please talk about it away from your home or wherever the ghost was. Talk in terms of the ghost being gone; talk about him having safely made the passage and say that he is now happily on the other side. Do not sound as if you miss the ghost or wish he were still there.

Some people do miss the activity or excitement of having a ghost in their life, and they unwittingly ask them to come back. If you miss your ghost, please find something else to fill up that empty space in your life. Both you and the ghost need to get on with your separate lives.

If you believe you might have more than one ghost, which is not uncommon, I would recommend going to the rooms where you suspect the ghosts are and repeating steps one through six.

Calling on the Squadron

About a year ago, my guides told me about a group of former earthbound spirits that have formed a group that calls itself the Squadron. Their job is to find earthbound spirits and bring them home to the other side. If you would prefer to call in the Squadron, rather than do the ghostbusting yourself, by all means do. All you need to do is ask the Squadron to come to your home and take the ghosts home with them. Even though you can't see them, they are serious about their work and will help out whenever asked. I would recommend burning some sage after you're done.

What to Do If Your Child Is Frightened

It is not uncommon for animals or for children up to the age of seven to see spirits. The reason children see spirits more frequently than we do is that their intellect isn't at work telling them that what they are seeing is impossible to see. They are still at that trusting age. What they see, they see. It's that simple.

You've probably heard the term "invisible friends"; they are not make-believe. Young kids are seeing either adult or children spirits. It's also not uncommon for the spirits of little children to play with living children.

Children can also see the guardian angels or deceased relatives who come to visit them. Sometimes deceased parents or grandparents will come by just to see how they're doing.

Dogs and cats can usually see these visiting entities as well. Cats will watch something floating around a room, and I have seen my dog walk over and sniff at something that wasn't physically there. I've also seen him growl at invisible things in a room. When I open up psychically to see what it is, there is usually an angel or someone deceased that I know standing there, and yet other times when I sense someone in the room, he might not react at all. I don't know why he can see some things and not others.

If your child complains that a ghost is trying to frighten her, don't be too quick to judge her as crazy or just exercising her wild imagination. Listen and ask questions. She may become too frightened to sleep in her own room or walk through the house without you by her side.

If something like this does occur, I have a great suggestion that was passed on to me by my therapist, who got it from someone she knew. It was originally for children who are frightened by monsters under the bed, but I wondered after she told me if it wouldn't also work for some of my little clients who are frightened by ghosts. Ironically, that same day I got a call from a parent whose five year old was frightened by a ghost he claimed was in the family home. Here was the suggestion I passed on to the mom:

Go buy the child a can of air freshener. Show him how to spray at the ghost with the can, while telling it to go to the light. Just keep spraying until the ghost goes away. What this does is help empower the child to feel that he is not powerless and can do something to get rid of this unwanted visitor.

The boy's mother called back about two weeks later and told me it worked like a charm. She said that he had always been frightened to go to the basement or attic by himself and would not go into any rooms without one of his parents with him. She said that since she got him the can of air freshener, he is now king of the house, he carries his can with him wherever he goes and now goes all throughout the house by himself.

Within a month of that phone call, I got two other phone calls from parents of small children, both saying their children were seeing ghosts and were very frightened because the ghosts weren't friendly. I told them about the air freshener and it worked with both of them also.

•   •   •

If your child is seeing ghosts and is afraid, try the air freshener. Make sure that as he is spraying the ghost, he tells him in a stern voice to leave and go to the light. This should help him feel empowered and no longer feel like the victim, which is so important. Remember, too, to keep it simple. Tell him that ghosts are lost souls who need guidance as to where to go and that he is doing a good thing by sending them to the light. Kids don't need any big heavy explanations of what this is all about. Just keep it simple.

What About Demons and Evil Spirits?

Some people are under the misconception that all ghosts are demonic or evil. In order for ghosts to be demonic or evil, they had to be that way in their life. We are in death the way we were in life, except that we are a little bit mellower and our perception of things changes. Who we are here is basically who we are there.

In all my years as a ghostbuster, I have never met a demonic spirit. I have met some pretty negative, hateful spirits, but nothing that I would call evil. Ghosts are souls. It is that simple.

One of my students asked me what evil spirits were, so I asked my guides for their definition. Here's what they had to say: "Unfortunately, there are many evil people on earth, people who have no regard for one another, perhaps who would love to see their fellow man fail, be hurt, tortured emotionally, mentally or physically. People who hate clear through to their soul. People who have no conscience, no morals. No desire for good. The problem is that these people die and are souls who may or may not choose to go on to the other side."

They gave me a mental picture of a group of these evil spirits who all hang out together. Then they said, "They always hang out with their own kind, whether they're in the body or out." There is a universal law, and that is *like attracts like.* Ghosts or spirits who hang around us will usually be similar to us. When we are living in the body, we hang out with other people who are similar to us in beliefs, morals, values. That doesn't change in death.

As for green-eyed, frothy-mouthed, orange-slimed, demonic monsters, that'll cost you about $7.00 and a little extra for popcorn and candy. *They're only in the movies!*

Afterword

AT THE RISK of sounding like a broken record, I really want you to get it that ghosts are souls of deceased people who have chosen not to go on to the other side. They are as varied as the people we see walking around on our planet, and each one of them has their reasons for choosing to stay here.

Souls have taught me a lot over the last thirty years in my work as a psychic, spiritual healer and ghostbuster. If you'd like to know more about the soul's perspective of life, death and life after death or would like to learn more about the realm most of us refer to as heaven, read my third book, *Echoes of the Soul* (New World Library). It will give you a deeper understanding of souls and why we do the things we do.

If you have a ghost story you would like to share with me (possibly for a future book) or would like information on my other books and tapes, you can check out my web site at www.echobodine.com or write to me at:

> Echo Bodine
> P.O. Box 385321,
> Bloomington, MN 55438

Thanks!